D1208169

A Field Guide to the
SNAKES
of BORNEO

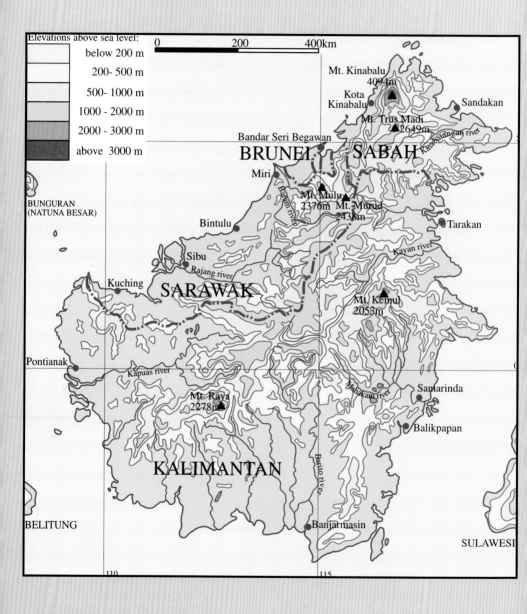

Map of Borneo.

A Field Guide to the
SNAKES
of BORNEO

Robert B. Stuebing and Robert F. Inger

with photographs by

R.B. Stuebing, R.F. Inger, C.L. Chan, I. Das, B. Lardner,
H.K. Voris, Stephen Von Peltz, John Murphy, Jimmy Omar,
Au Kam Wah, R. Cutter, D.R. Karns, A. Lamb, Francis Lim,
W.M. Poon, D. Wechsler and Yong Hoi Sen

and illustrations by

Tan Fui Lian

Natural History Publications (Borneo)
Kota Kinabalu

1999

Published by

Natural History Publications (Borneo) Sdn. Bhd.
A913, 9th Floor, Wisma Merdeka,
P.O. Box 13908,
88846 Kota Kinabalu, Sabah, Malaysia.
Tel: 6088-233098 Fax: 6088-240768
e-mail: chewlun@tm.net.my

Text copyright © 1999 Natural History Publications (Borneo) Sdn. Bhd.
Photographs and illustrations copyright © 1999 as credited.

All rights reserved. No part of this publication may be reproduced,
stored in a retrieval system, or transmitted in any form or by any
means, electronic, mechanical, photocopying, recording, or otherwise,
without the prior permission of the copyright owners.

First published 1999

A Field Guide to the Snakes of Borneo
by Robert B. Stuebing and Robert F. Inger

Half title page: *Trimeresurus malcolmi.* (Photo: R.B. Stuebing)
Facing Foreword: *Ahaetulla prasina.* (Photo: C.L. Chan)

Design and layout by C.L. Chan

Perpustakaan Negara Malaysia Cataloguing-in-Publication Data

Stuebing, Robert
    A field guide to the snakes of Borneo / Robert Stuebing
    and Robert Inger with photographs by R.B. Stuebing.
    [et al.] ; and illustrations by Tan Fui Lian.
    Bibliography : p. 241.
    Includes index
    ISBN 983-812-031-6 (Softcover)
    ISBN 983-812-038-3 (Hardcover)
    1. Snakes—Borneo. 2. Snakes—Classification.
    I. Inger, Robert. II. Chan, C.L. III. Tan, Fui Lian. IV. Title.
    597.96095983

Printed in Malaysia

Contents

C.L. Chan

Foreword

S nakes have always had a special part in the human psyche, although perhaps usually thought of in a somewhat negative light. That this is a group of animals often poorly understood, and certainly even less often studied carefully, is a key message of this account.

More importantly, the main aspects of their diversity, how snakes fit into nature and how, indeed, they serve people in their principal role as predators, are significant topics that require both appreciation and understanding. In natural history, which is integral and basic to a fuller awareness of nature and the need for its conservation, the story of snakes is as important and intriguing as that of any other major faunal group. The story of their life habits, their adaptations to special habitats and niches, and in a number of instances their rarity, fits in well with our picture of the tropical rain forest—where life forms abound and those able to compete successfully or develop special niches for themselves are those that survive.

That we have specialists willing to tell snake stories in this form enriches our own lives and culture, and furnishes yet another milestone in the story of nature in our midst. Borneo, as many will testify, is incredibly rich in nature. This, in turn, means that our relative understanding of the many aspects of nature—given that few specialists exist for each of the multitudinous groups of plants and animals (and perhaps the necessity to view the importance of biological documentation on a diminishing time scale) is still inadequate. That the story of snakes can be told for Borneo, and told in the present form, is a worthy accomplishment indeed.

Chong Kah Kiat
Minister of Tourism Development, Environment,
Science and Technology,
Sabah

A. Lamb

Introduction

The island of Borneo covers an area of about 575,000 sq km, making it roughly 85% the size of the State of Texas in the U.S.A. Despite Borneo's smaller size, its equatorial location makes it far richer in species than comparable areas outside the tropics. As for its snake fauna, Borneo outstrips Texas about three to one. Until the early part of this century, more than three-quarters of Borneo was covered by forests of some kind, from mangrove and peat swamp, to lowland forests dominated by the magnificent giant trees of the Family Dipterocapaceae, and the relatively less extensive oak and coniferous forests of higher altitudes. Some mountains, such as the famous Mount Kinabalu in Sabah, have significant amounts of truly montane vegetation. The tremendous variety of topography and vegetation in Borneo has provided an almost endless range of habitats for snakes to exploit, and so the latter are found almost everywhere on land, and in coastal seas as well.

Research on Bornean snakes has been rather limited, and little was published on the subject until one of the authors (RFI) began systematic research on the Borneo herpetofauna beginning in the late 1950s. Prior to that, the best reference work available was written by Nellie De Rooij, a Dutch scientist at the Leiden Museum in the Netherlands, published in 1917! This book is a primary reference still considered extremely useful by all students of Bornean herpetology to this day. Other works worth noting are the checklists produced in 1950 by De Haas (as part of a larger work on the reptiles of the Indo-Malesian Archipelago) and the first checklist and key devoted entirely to Bornean snakes by Neville Haile, a most talented geologist who worked in Sarawak in the 1950s and 60s. Specialised research

---

(Opposite). Batu Lawi, the highlands of Borneo.

1

on particular groups such as the genus *Calamaria*, have been done by Robert F. Inger and H. Marx, but little if any of this work has been available, or written in such a way as to be accessible to ordinary people, including visitors to Borneo, with an enthusiasm for snakes. Our first experiment along these lines was a publication entitled *Frogs of Sabah*, a little illustrated field guide with the amateur naturalist in mind. In the same spirit, we have attempted to make identification of Bornean snakes a bit easier for those who are non-specialists, but still have a keen interest. In this book, to make identification an easier task, we have presented photographs of individual species wherever possible. However, as anyone who has worked with snakes in Borneo already knows, many are quite difficult to identify based solely on a photograph, so we have included a key and a species description to improve chances for accurate identification. Nevertheless, some groups remain notoriously difficult for both amateurs and professionals alike, such as the reed snakes (*Calamaria*) and the sea snakes (Hydrophiinae). Considerable work is still required to make these groups really accessible. Also, the current list of Bornean snakes is certainly not final, as new species continue to be found.

Work on this book is based on about 35 years of fieldwork in Borneo, and museum visits in Malaysia, Singapore and Field Museum, Chicago, U.S.A. There have been a few harrowing moments, but these are far outweighed by the privilege of witnessing firsthand the extraordinarily beautiful biological diversity of Borneo, and enjoying the warmth and generosity of its people.

Classification and Diversity of the Snakes of Borneo

S nakes first appear in the fossil record about 150 million years ago during the Jurassic Period of the Mesozoic Era. The "ruling" reptiles of that period were the archosaurs, which included the dinosaurs. Crocodiles and birds are the descendants of this once dominant group, while the majority of today's reptiles are members of the Order Squamata, meaning, "scaly", referring to the distinctive scales of their skin. The dinosaurs abruptly died out towards the end of the Cretaceous Period (about 80 million years ago), an event that many scientists now believe was caused by the collision of a giant meteor or asteroid with the Earth. Most reptiles that remained were either small, or lived in habitats where the temperature did not vary much. Snakes, which were probably living either underground or in sheltered habitats, survived well.

While most other vertebrates have made good use of their limbs, snakes evidently lost theirs rather early in their evolutionary history, during a time when their ancestors lived underground. Snakes are thought to have been derived from limbed, lizard-like reptiles, since fossil lizards predate those of snakes. Furthermore, some snakes such as blind snakes and pythons still retain remnants of hind limbs. In pythons, the latter are still visible externally as a small pair of claws located on either side of the anus.

This trend towards the loss of limbs is evident in some modern lizard groups also. The Scincidae (skinks), for example, have numerous species whose legs are much reduced in size, and some whose legs have been lost altogether. *Ophisaurus büttikoferi*, a Bornean lizard of the family Anguidae, lacks legs entirely, and sometimes is referred to as a "glass snake", since it closely resembles a snake. However, like many lizards, its tail breaks off easily (a process called "autotomy") and can regenerate, an ability not found in snakes.

Locomotion in snakes depends on modifications in the body skeleton and musculature. The number of vertebrae (individual elements of the backbone) and their associated ribs has been increased so that pythons, for example, possess around 400 vertebrae and more than 300 pairs of ribs.

Some scientists have suggested that a model for the ancestors of snakes can be found in the famous "cicak purba" or earless monitor (*Lanthonotus borneensis*) of Sarawak and West Kalimantan. This odd species is not actually related to monitor lizards, but has been placed tentatively in the family Helodermatidae (along with the American Gila Monster, *Heloderma suspectum*). *Lanthonotus* has no eyelids or external ears, and lives underground in swampy areas. Unfortunately, because of its apparent rarity, little is known of its life history.

Snakes are a suborder of the Squamata called the Serpentes ("Ophidia", in some texts). Both words mean "snakes", and in Borneo there is a total of ten[1] families with at least 154 species (See page 9). There is a great diversity of form, size and lifestyle in Bornean snakes, from primitive burrowers to the most advanced group, the vipers. About one-third of the fauna is endemic to the island, e.g., found nowhere else. The greatest faunal similarity is shared with Sumatra and Peninsular Malaysia.

The Typhlopidae, or blind snakes, have been placed in the oldest known snake group, the Scolecophidia. All these species are blind burrowers with rudimentary, scale-covered eyes and no enlarged ventral scales. Teeth are present only in the upper jaw. Most species are less than about 10 cm in length, though the largest, the Striped Blind Snake (*Ramphotyphlops lineatus*) reaches half a metre in total length. Interestingly, the common blind snake, *Rhamphotyphlops braminus*, is parthenogenetic, meaning that females lay eggs that develop normally in the absence of males.

Two other lineages that are regarded as rather old among snakes are the pipe snakes (Cylindrophiidae and Anomochilidae) and pythons (Pythonidae). The former two are small-eyed burrowers thought to have been in existence for at least 50 million years. Except for the Common Pipe Snake, *Cylindrophis ruffus*, most members of these families are known from only a few specimens, and sometimes only one. Their habits are extremely secretive so that encounters with them are rare; thus, new species continue to be found. On the other hand, pythons are among the most well-known snakes in the world. They are regarded as "primitive" because of some skeletal features

---

[1] Typhlopidae, Anomochilidae, Cylindrophiidae, Pythonidae, Xenopeltidae, Xenophidiidae, Acrochordidae, Colubridae, Elapidae, Viperaidae.

and the remnants of hind limbs. No pythons in Borneo are burrowers, though there are related species elsewhere in the world that retain the burrowing habit. The Reticulate Python (*Python reticulatus*), is quite common in Borneo and probably holds the record for the largest snake species at 9.83 metres in total length. Specimens approaching this length are now extremely rare, though four to six metre reticulate pythons are relatively common.

The Xenopeltidae, or earth snakes, superficially resemble pipe snakes, though there is but one known species in the family. *Xenopeltis* is known for the beautiful diffraction colours of the rainbow shimmering from its glossy black scales.

The Xenophidiidae is a newly recognized family, established late in 1998 and based on only two species of uncertain relations. The single Bornean species, *Xenophidion acanthognathus*, was found just a few years ago and was described in 1997. A spine-like bony process protruding from its lower jaw is a puzzling structure whose function is unknown.

The file snakes (Acrochordidae) have a primitive reptilian character, the presence of bony elements incorporated into individual scales. In *Acrochordus*, there is a raised knot, or denticle, in the centre of each scale, making the texture of the skin extremely rough or abrasive. The acrochordids are something of a mystery group since they have no known living, or even fossil relatives. The "elephant's trunk snake" (*A. javanicus*) is common in Sarawak and West Kalimantan, though surprisingly it has not yet been found in Sabah. In contrast, the marine file snake, *A. granulatus*, is common in shallow coastal waters throughout Borneo.

The largest and most varied group of snakes in Borneo is the family Colubridae. Colubrids are thought to have appeared from 35–50 million years ago, and display a remarkable array of forms and lifestyles. No single trait has yet been found to unite them all, and scientists who study snake systematics remain puzzled about the relationships between the various subfamilies, of which there are six in Borneo.

The Homalopsinae is an assortment of mostly aquatic snakes, typically blunt-headed, with protruding beady eyes and crescent-shaped, valvular nostrils located on the upper surface of the head. All of the homalopsinae are rear-fanged (*opisthoglyphous*) and mildly venomous. None are apparently dangerous to humans, however, since no serious or life-threatening symptoms have ever been reported from the bite of a homalopsine[2]. The most common species of this group are the brackish water Dog-Faced Water Snake

---

[2] See Chapter 3: Snakes and People in Borneo.

5

(*Cerberus rynchops*) and the Orange-Bellied Mud Snake (*Enhydris plumbea*).

The subfamily Xenoderminae, of which there are two Bornean species, have strongly keeled or knobbed scales and many more scale rows than most colubrids. A rare montane member of this group, *Stoliczkaia borneensis*, is unusual within the family in having more than 30 dorsal scale rows.

The Pareatinae are mostly snakes of the forest floor or understorey. Most are small and inconspicuous, and one species actually mimics dead twigs or branches. *Pareas*, generally found near the forest floor, is distinct in having no mental groove on the underside of the lower jaw, which is normally present in most other snakes. The Blunt-Headed Tree Snake, *Aplopeltura boa*, has a protrusible lower jaw and a rigid posture which augments its camouflaged pattern.

The Lycodontinae, or wolf snakes, as the name suggests, possess several enlarged teeth, as do the genera *Oligodon* ("kukri" snakes) and *Psammodynastes* ("mock vipers"). *Oligodon* has eight species in Borneo, which seems to be the major centre of diversity for this group. The *Psammodynastes* apparently mimic true vipers with their triangular head shape and aggressive-looking "strike" posture.

The largest and most diverse group of the colubrids is the subfamily Colubrinae. The genera of this groups are too numerous to be mentioned individually, but several are noteworthy.

Snakes of the genus *Boiga* (arboreal "cat-snakes") unlike most other colubrids have a vertical, or cat-like pupil. They can attain a total length of two metres or more. The head is triangular, and much broader than the neck, while the teeth are long, curved and enlarged posteriorly, giving these snakes a rather formidable, viper-like appearance.

Borneo has been a major centre of speciation for the *Calamaria*, or reed snakes, small colubrines of the leaf litter. They are distinguished from other ground snakes by a lack of prefrontal scales, and extremely short, pointed tails. At least 22 species occur in Borneo, and at least two-thirds of them occur in Sabah and Sarawak. Six are known exclusively from Mount Kinabalu.

The genus *Chrysopelea* forms a small but notable genus of colubrids in Borneo, and includes the famous "flying" Paradise Tree Snake. These beautifully patterned snakes are mostly arboreal, and have the ability to flatten their bodies sufficiently to glide from the treetops if danger threatens. They are equipped with a mild venom which is, however, not dangerous to humans.

Snakes of the genus *Elaphe* in Borneo are generally referred to as racers, and possess a highly characteristic body cross-section resembling that of a loaf of bread. All the *Elaphe* and their close relatives (e.g., *Gonyosoma*, *Gonyophis*) are constrictors and climb well, using the angled edges of their ventral scales to anchor themselves on irregularities of the branches or rock ledges which they climb. They range from the common dark-coloured racer of disturbed lowland areas (*Elaphe flavolineata*) to the strikingly beautiful resident of the forest canopy, the orange-banded Royal Tree Snake (*Gonyophis margaritatus*). Most racers have prominent eyes, and the largest eyes are found in the White-Bellied Rat Snake, *Zaocys fuscus*. Large *Zaocys* can at first glance be mistaken for a King Cobra because of the former's colour and "fierce" stare. The head of the King Cobra is much shorter and broader than that of any of the racers. Also, all racers are of course non-venomous, though their bite can be painful.

Another subfamily of snakes frequently encountered in the forested or aquatic habitats of Borneo are the Natricinae. Most have moderately to heavily keeled scales, and enlarged rear teeth, and some have a distinct groove down the back of the head and neck, which has been found to contain venom glands. Although some natricines from South-east Asia, such as *Rhabdophis* species in southern China, are known to possess a venomous bite, none in Borneo have ever been reported to have caused toxic effects in humans. Caution is, however, advised. At the very least, the large rear "fangs" of snakes (e.g., *Macropisthodon*) can inflict a painful wound. *Amphiesma* and *Rhabdophis* are the most common natricine genera in Borneo.

The remaining two Bornean families include numerous species which are venomous and potentially dangerous. The Elapidae (13 genera and 19 species) are a diverse group in the Sunda region, composed of three subfamilies, the terrestrial Elapinae (cobras, kraits and "coral" snakes), the amphibious Laticaudinae, or sea kraits and the fully aquatic (marine) Hydrophiinae. All elapids have short, thorn-like fangs rigidly fixed to the upper jaw or maxilla. The gape is small, and most elapids have difficulty biting any broad, flat surface. Though the types of venoms and toxicity vary somewhat, all cobras possess neurotoxic (nerve-poison) elements causing paralysis. The sea snakes possess additional *myotoxins*, which digest and incapacitate muscle cells and *erabutoxins* which destroy nerve-muscle connections.

The Elapinae can be strikingly coloured (*Bungarus*, *Maticora*) and often exhibit conspicuous threat or warning behaviour. Kraits and coral snakes are secretive in their habits, but if disturbed display a brightly coloured tail or belly. The reactions of cobras (*Naja, Ophiophagus*) to disturbance is well known. They expand or flatten the ribs of the neck while hissing or blowing menacingly. The King Cobra (*Ophiophagus hannah*) can reach up to five metres in length, and should always be treated as deadly. The Sumatran Cobra is also rather dangerous, since in addition to biting, this species can also emit venom from its modified fangs, in a fine spray up to about one metre.

The true sea snakes (all of which are venomous), are easily distinguished by their flattened, oar-shaped tails, and can be divided further into to two sub-families in Borneo. The sea-kraits (genus *Laticauda*), regularly come ashore. *Laticauda* have well developed ventral scales similar to those of land snakes. Yellow-lipped sea kraits (*Laticauda colubrina*) are common on many small rocky islands or outcrops off the west coasts of Sabah and Sarawak. On "Snake Island" (Pulau Kalampunian Damit near Pulau Tiga Park), up to 150 individual sea kraits can be found on any given day. Their ventral scales enable these snakes to occasionally climb several metres up into trees.

The second group of marine snakes includes all fully aquatic genera (*Hydrophis, Leioselasma, Enhydrina, Lapemis, Aipysurus* and others). While most sea snakes have partially or completely lost the specialised ventrals, hydrophiines still possess a ventral fold, an adaptation to flatten the body from side to side for swimming. All sea snakes are potentially dangerous, despite their tiny fangs, since the potency of their venom can be from two to five times that of a cobra.

There are six species of Crotalidae (pit-vipers) in Borneo, and all but two of these are relatively common. Most have keeled scales, broad triangular heads and rather thin necks. Juveniles are light green or brown, while adults usually have a pattern of dark crossbands on a yellowish or greenish background. Crotalids have extremely long, recurved fangs which are hinged at the front of the upper jaw and folded into the mouth when not in use. These *solenoglyphous* teeth can be erected almost instantaneously and plunged into a victim to inject substantial quantities of haemotoxic venom (acting on blood vessels and elements). Based on what is known of pit-vipers elsewhere in the world, the venom is probably a mixture of diverse enzymes, and some local crotalids (such as *Trimeresurus popeorum* or *Ovophis chaseni*) may possess neurotoxic elements in their venom. Thus, all vipers should be treated with a considerable respect. Bornean crotalids are nocturnal, locate prey primarily using the conspicuous heat-sensing pits located between the eye and the nostril. The largest species, *Trimeresurus sumatranus*, attains a maximum total length of about 1.5 metres, and like other crotalids, is increasingly stout-bodied at larger sizes. The most beautiful crotalid in Borneo is the heavy-bodied and elegantly coloured Kinabalu Pit-Viper, *Trimeresurus malcolmi.*

A Checklist of the Snakes of Borneo

Typhlopidae
Ramphotyphlops braminus (Daudin)
Ramphotyphlops lineatus Boie
Ramphotyphlops lorenzi Werner*
Ramphotyphlops olivaceus (Gray)
Typhlops koekoeki Brongersma*
Typhlops muelleri Schlegel

Cylindrophiidae
Cylindrophis engkariensis Stuebing*
Cylindrophis lineatus Blanford
Cylindrophis ruffus[3] Laurenti

Anomochilidae
Anomochilus leonardi Smith
Anomochilus weberi Lidth de Jeude

Pythonidae
Python curtus Schlegel
Python reticulatus (Schneider)

Xenopeltidae
Xenopeltis unicolor Reinwardt

Xenophidiidae
Xenophidion acanthognathus Gunther & Manthey*

---

* endemic species.
[3] Most books list this as *Cylindrophis rufus.*

9

Acrochordidae
Acrochordus granulatus (Schneider)
Acrochordus javanicus Hornstedt

Colubridae
Xenodermatinae
Stoliczkaia borneensis Boulenger*
Xenelaphis ellipsifer Boulenger
Xenelaphis hexagonotus (Cantor)
Xenodermus javanicus Reinhardt

Pareatinae
Aplopeltura boa (H. Boie)
Pareas carinatus (Boie)
Pareas laevis (Boie)
Pareas malaccanus (Peters)
Pareas nuchalis (Boulenger)*
Pareas vertebralis (Boulenger)

Homalopsinae
Cerberus rynchops (Schneider)
Enhydris alternans (Reuss)
Enhydris doriae (Peters)*
Enhydris enhydris (Schneider)
Enhydris plumbea (Boie)
Enhydris punctata (Gray)
Fordonia leucobalia (Schlegel)
Homalopsis buccata (Linnaeus)

Lycodontinae
Lepturophis borneensis Boulenger
Lycodon albofuscus (Duméril, Bibron & Duméril)
Lycodon aulicus (Linnaeus)
Lycodon effraenis Cantor
Lycodon subcinctus H. Boie
Oligodon annulifer Boulenger*
Oligodon cinereus (Günther)
Oligodon everetti Boulenger*
Oligodon octolineatus (Schneider)

Oligodon purpurascens (Schlegel)
Oligodon signatus (Günther)*
Oligodon subcarinatus (Günther)
Oligodon vertebralis (Günther)
Psammodynastes pictus Günther
Psammodynastes pulverulentus (Boie)

Colubrinae
Ahaetulla fasciolata (Fischer)
Ahaetulla prasina (Boie)
Boiga cynodon[4] (Boie)
Boiga dendrophila (Boie)
Boiga drapiezii (Boie)
Boiga jaspidea (Duméril, Bibron & Duméril)
Boiga nigriceps (Günther)
Calamaria battersbyi Inger & Marx
Calamaria bicolor Duméril Bibron & Duméril
Calamaria borneensis Bleeker*
Calamaria everetti Boulenger
Calamaria gervaisii Duméril, Bibron & Duméril
Calamaria grabowskii Fischer*
Calamaria gracillima (Günther)
Calamaria griswoldi Loveridge*
Calamaria hilleniusi Inger & Marx*
Calamaria lateralis Mocquard*
Calamaria leucogaster Bleeker
Calamaria lovi Boulenger
Calamaria lumbricoidea Boie
Calamaria lumholtzi Andersson*
Calamaria melanota Jan*
Calamaria modesta Duméril, Bibron & Duméril
Calamaria prakkei van Lidth de Jeude
Calamaria rebentischi Bleeker*
Calamaria schlegelii Duméril, Bibron & Duméril
Calamaria schmidti Marx & Inger
Calamaria suluensis Taylor

---

[4] *Boiga cyanea* has been reported from western Sarawak, but the record has not been confirmed.

Calamaria virgulata Boie
Chrysopelea paradisi Boie
Chrysopelea pelias (Linnaeus)
Dendrelaphis caudolineatus (Gray)
Dendrelaphis formosus (Boie)
Dendrelaphis pictus (Gmelin)
Dryocalamus subannulatus (Duméril, Bibron & Duméril)
Dryocalamus tristrigatus Günther*
Dryophiops rubescens (Gray)
Elaphe erythrura (Duméril, Bibron & Duméril)
Elaphe flavolineata (Schlegel)
Elaphe radiata (Boie)
Elaphe taeniura Cope
Gonyophis margaritatus (Peters)
Gonyosoma oxycephalum (Boie)
Liopeltis baliodeirus Boie
Liopeltis longicauda (Peters)
Liopeltis tricolor (Schlegel)
Pseudorabdion albonuchalis (Günther)*
Pseudorabdion collaris (Mocquard)*
Pseudorabdion longiceps (Cantor)
Pseudorabdion saravacensis (Shelford)
Sibynophis geminatus (H. Boie)
Sibynophis melanocephalus (Gray)
Stegonotus borneensis Inger*
Zaocys carinatus (Günther)
Zaocys fuscus (Günther)

Natricinae
Amphiesma flavifrons (Boulenger)*
Amphiesma frenata (Dunn)*
Amphiesma petersi (Boulenger)
Amphiesma saravacensis (Günther)
Hydrablabes periops (Günther)*
Hydrablabes praefrontalis (Mocquard)
Macropisthodon flaviceps (Dumeril & Bibron)
Macropisthodon rhodomelas (Boie)
Opisthotropis typica (Mocquard)*
Oreocalamus hanitschi Boulenger

Pseudoxenodon baramensis (Smith)*
Rhabdophis chrysarga (Schlegel)
Rhabdophis conspicillata (Günther)
Rhabdophis murudensis (Smith)*
Xenochrophis maculata (Edeling)
Xenochrophis trianguligera (Boie)

Elapidae
Elapinae

Bungarus fasciatus (Schneider)
Bungarus flaviceps Reinhardt
Maticora bivirgata (Boie)
Maticora intestinalis (Laurenti)
Naja sumatrana Mueller
Ophiophagus hannah (Cantor)

Laticaudinae

Laticauda colubrina (Schneider)
Laticauda laticaudata (Linnaeus)

Hydrophiinae

Aipysurus eydouxii (Gray)
Enhydrina schistosa (Daudin)
Hydrophis brookii Günther
Hydrophis caerulescens (Shaw)
Hydrophis fasciatus (Schneider)
Hydrophis klossi Boulenger
Hydrophis melanosoma Günther
Hydrophis ornatus (Gray)
Hydrophis torquatus (Günther)
Kerilia jerdoni Gray
Kolpophis annandalei Gray
Lapemis curtus Shaw
Leioselasma cyanocincta (Daudin)
Leioselasma spiralis (Shaw)
Microcephalophis gracilis (Shaw)
Pelamis platurus (Linnaeus)
Praescutata viperina (Schmidt)
Thalassophis anomalus Schmidt

13

Crotalidae

Ovophis chaseni (Smith)*
Trimeresurus borneensis (Peters)*
Trimeresurus malcolmi Loveridge*
Trimeresurus popeorum Smith
Trimeresurus sumatranus (Raffles)
Tropidolaemus wagleri (Boie)

Adaptations and Ecology of Bornean Snakes

orneo is home to some of the richest biological diversity on earth. Its snake fauna contributes significantly to this phenomenon. On land, snakes live in the lowlands and the mountains, in the soil, in leaf litter, on the ground as well as at every level above ground. In aquatic habitats, they live in ponds, rocky streams, turbid rivers, and are abundant in the shallow coastal seas. Species can be as thin as a shoelace and as short as a pencil, or as thick as a human thigh and over nine metres long.

Apparently, snake ancestors developed numerous anatomical peculiarities as a result of their "fossorial" (underground) lifestyle, including the loss of eyelids and legs, and specialisation of the ribs and their associated complex musculature. A typical land snake will crawl by temporarily anchoring the edges of transverse ventral scales against objects in the environment, such as protruding edges or surface irregularities. These provide leverage for the snake to pull itself along on consecutive pairs of ribs. Although the speed is rather slow, usually only a fraction of a metre per second, within dense or tangled habitats a snake will appear to travel swiftly. The function of ventral scales becomes more obvious if we observe the great difficulty with which a blind snake or hydrophiine sea snake crawls on land. Both lack the broad ventrals of the majority of land snakes.

The eyes and ears of snakes have also changed apparently as a result of the life-style of their ancestors. The internal structure of the eye has been reorganised considerably. In mammals and some other vertebrates, contractions of surrounding muscles change the shape of a disc-shaped lens. The snake lens is spherical, and moves in or out to focus an image on the retina. Interestingly, colour vision in snakes has not been lost. Snakes possess no eyelids, but instead a hard, clear shield called a "brille" that is shed with the head skin. In addition, snakes have no external ears, and apart from the ability to sense low frequency vibrations through solid substrates, are essentially deaf. Burrowing animals have little use for eyelids or external ears. (The glass snake above gives away its identity as a lizard because it possesses both.)

The characteristics of the internal organs have also changed to fit a long and narrow body. Kidneys have been placed not together, but staggered, with (usually) the right one further forward than the left. The stomach is long and followed by a similar-looking intestine. Since all snakes are carnivorous, they do not require a long coiled intestine as would be found in a herbivorous animal.

A more noticeable difference can be seen in the organs of breathing, where we find that only a few snakes still possess a pair of lungs, and the majority retain only an elongated right lung. Interestingly, fully aquatic snakes such as the Hydrophiinae (sea snakes) which dive or otherwise spend a considerable amount of time submerged have developed an expanded or "saccular" lung extending almost the length of the body and into the tail. These snakes can also "breathe" while submerged by absorbing oxygen dissolved in the water through the thin skin linking their scales. In contrast, file snakes have overcome the respiratory challenge of submersion by increasing their blood volume. Marine file snakes (*Acrochordus granulatus*), common in shallow coastal waters off Sabah and Sarawak, have extremely efficient hemoglobin and also can breathe by absorbing oxygen through the skin.

About one-third of all Bornean snakes still live either partially or completely under the surface of the soil, in leaf litter or under the bark of dead trees and rotten logs. The genera *Ramphotyphlops* and *Typhlops* (blind snakes), *Anomochilus* and *Cylindrophis* (pipe snakes) are all secretive burrowers and rarely seen. The most commonly encountered of all of them is the non-native blind snake, *Ramphotyphlops braminus*, which finds its way into potted plants or flower beds and is often washed out by heavy rains. These snakes resemble shiny black earthworms, but can easily be distinguished from the latter by their glossy black (scaly) skin, and the fact that they wriggle side to side, and cannot contract their bodies as they crawl. Their skin is also hard, dry and glossy, and not soft and moist like that of an earthworm. Blind snakes and pipe snakes have tiny, rudimentary eyes (covered by scales in the Typhlopidae), and most have lost all traces of enlarged ventral scales.

The *Calamaria* are a group of colubrids that seek their livelihood not in soils, but in leaf litter. There are over 20 known species in Borneo, and all are similar in shape and lifestyle, with narrow heads (and fully formed eyes) and a short sharp tail. None exceed about 25 cm in length. Joining the *Calamaria* in the leaf-litter community are genera such as *Pareas, Pseudorabdion* and *Dryocalamus*, to name a few. They are joined on the forest floor by several venomous (and dangerous) genera, such as *Maticora, Bungarus* and *Trimeresurus*. The latter, which attain a much larger size than *Calamaria*, often feed on small vertebrates.

All snakes eat animal prey of one sort or another, and no species are even partially herbivorous. Interestingly, since they have lost much of the olfactory (sense of smell) sensors of their nasal passages, snakes locate their prey through "taste", by sampling the air or substrate with the tongue, and placing the tongue tip in the specialised "vomeronasal organ" in the roof of the mouth. This sensing system is quite useful to burrowers who can neither see nor hear their prey.

In forests, caves or open areas the rat snakes and racers (*Elaphe, Gonyosoma, Gonyophis, Zaocys* and others) as well as cobras (*Naja* and *Ophiophagus*) hunt in daylight, preying mostly on birds or small mammals. Generally, their large eyes with round pupils are used in bright light, though *Elaphe taeniata* hunts bats deep in caves. There are several specialised adaptations for prey capture. Rat snakes and "racers" use constriction to kill prey, which is approached either through stealth or by patient waiting. Cobras and their relatives hunt down their victims in burrows or nests and envenom the prey, which die rapidly from paralysis of respiratory and heart muscles.

Most nocturnal snakes (pythons, vipers) use non-visual cues to locate and capture prey. Though their eyes do possess cat-like, vertical pupils, and are able to function in quite dim light, both pythons and crotalid vipers rely on heat-sensitive pits which detect changes as small as one-thousandth of a degree Celsius. Needless to say, any object such as a small warm-blooded animal can be precisely detected even while the snake remains motionless. Pythons rely on stealth, long curved teeth and quick constriction to subdue their prey. Vipers, like elapids, possess enzyme-rich saliva, forming a deadly venom. The snake strikes a victim, and waits for it to collapse (usually within minutes), then locates it through a combination of odor cues and infrared heat.

Numerous forest snakes are at least partially arboreal, feeding from just above ground all the way into the canopy. In disturbed areas, or at the forest edge, snakes such as *Ahaetulla prasina* (with its curious horizontal pupils and binocular vision) and *Dendrelaphis caudolineatus* feed primarily on lizards. Cat snakes (genus *Boiga*), nocturnal predators of the understorey, feed on frogs, birds and other small vertebrates. Crotalids such as the Sumatran Pit-viper, common in palms, low shrubs and other vegetation within a few metres of the forest floor, feed mostly on birds and rodents. Some snakes, such as the beautiful Paradise Tree Snake (*Chrysopelea paradisi*) and the Royal Tree Snake (*Gonyophis margaritatus*), venture far into the canopy to feed on small vertebrates. The actual number of snake species feeding high up in the trees is unknown, since all herpetologists until now have always worked on the ground. Perhaps some of the new canopy walkways in various parts of Borneo will help to expand our knowledge in this area.

Other distinctive snake communities can be found in freshwater habitats such as swamps, pools, rivers and streams. (There are few naturally isolated lakes in Malaysian Borneo, except for swamps[5] or oxbow lakes associated with rivers). In lotic habitats with a constant current, natricines or the "true" water snakes are among the most visible residents. White-nosed juveniles of *Amphiesma flavifrons* are frequently seen during the day in upland, rocky rivers and streams, while at night, *Xenochrophis trianguligera* is relatively common. *Hydrablabes periops* is a more secretive, but nevertheless abundant water snake. Most of these snakes feed on tadpoles, fish, frogs, or frog eggs.

Swampy habitats are inhabited by glossy snakes such as *Xenopeltis unicolor* (rice fields) and *Enhydris plumbea* (buffalo wallows), which feed on frogs and tadpoles. These species are only rarely seen, since they live in clumps or mats of vegetation or under the overhanging bank of a flooded ricefield or wallow. Snakes of coastal mangroves are more conspicuously abundant. *Cerberus rynchops*, the Dog-Faced Water Snake, hunts on the shallow edge of an incoming tide, where it feeds on mudskippers and other small fishes. One night's search on a tidal mud flat on Sabah's west coast, near a village called Kampung Giling Laut, yielded over 70 individuals of this snake.

Deeper coastal waters are home to the sea snakes (Hydrophiinae), which have a great diversity of feeding habits. Many are rather specialised, such as the tiny headed *Microcephalophis gracilis* and *Hydrophis caerulescens*, adapted to entering the narrow burrows of gobies or other narrow-bodied fishes, and feeding on the trapped residents. In Marudu Bay, a shallow inlet in northern Sabah, large numbers of these goby-feeding *Hydrophis*

---

[5] The largest of these is the collection of swampy lakes called Danau Sentarum, in the upper Kapuas River, West Kalimantan.

caerulescens and *Hydrophis fasciatus* occur. *Aipysurus eydouxii*, common along Sabah's west coast, feeds entirely on fish eggs. Open water or pelagic species such as the large (up to three metres) *Leioselasma cyanocincta* are specialised in their diet, and feed exclusively on large eels (such as *Muraenesox* spp.). In contrast, the Short Sea Snake (*Lapemis curtus*) is one of the few generalist feeders among sea snakes, and hunts near the mouths of muddy rivers, taking over 30 different species of fish. All elapid sea snakes except *Laticauda* are rather helpless on land because of the loss of specialised ventral scales.

Because all snakes are limbless carnivores, many specialised anatomical and behavioural adaptations for feeding have been developed for seizing, killing and swallowing food. The most commonly seen approach involves either motionless "sit and wait" tactics or stealth followed by an instantaneous strike. Constriction or envenomation follows. Constrictors immediately pin the prey against a hard substrate and loop at least one coil about the victim's chest. The chest cavity is progressively compressed, with new force applied each time the prey animal exhales. Death is usually swift, and contrary to some popular opinions, the prey is never "crushed", but suffocated. Blood may flow from ruptured capillaries in the nose, however, giving the impression that internal damage has occurred. Swallowing begins once the prey has ceased to struggle, and almost always begins at the head (small prey may be swallowed backwards). The recurved teeth of all snakes are attached to jaw bones of high mobility, which can "walk" over the surface of the food item to force it backwards into the snake's throat. The tooth-bearing bones, lower jaw hinges at the front and rear, and some of the bones of the head are all attached by ligaments of great flexibility, allowing the snake's gape and throat to be expanded enormously (called jaw "kinesis"). Most of us have read accounts of pythons swallowing pigs, deer or other large animals, occasionally even people. In fact, all snakes possess this highly-developed swallowing ability. The crotalid vipers make further use of specialised jaw hinges in striking their prey. Their jaws can be opened to the extend that the poison fangs point directly forwards, and enable them to "stab" the prey without actually having to deliver a bite.

Sea snakes frequently seek out prey animals in burrows, or in the nooks and crannies of coral reefs. The fish or eel is bitten on the head, and in the case of the sea krait (*Laticauda colubrina*), the snake will then retire some distance away for up to 15 minutes, waiting for the victim's struggles to cease. The wisdom of this action is readily apparent, since moray eels are undoubtedly hazardous to the snake as long as they remain alive. Once the eel is dead, however, *Laticauda colubrina* moves in and will swallow a half-metre length moray eel in as little as seven seconds.

The dog-faced water snake has developed an interesting technique of its own: the snake approaches parallel to the prey (a fish or crab) and makes a sidewise lunge, pinning the victim against a convex loop of the snake's body and beginning the swallowing process almost immediately.

Small snakes form a key trophic group in Borneo's tropical forests as major predators within the leaf-litter community, and many species are specialists on particular food items. All are non-poisonous, and feed on earthworms, slugs or spiders. For example, the snakes of the genus *Pareas* and *Aplopeltura* eat snails or slugs, while similar-sized *Calamaria* eat earthworms, and *Liopeltis* eat only spiders! The ecological role of these small vertebrates (including small species of lizards) in the dynamics of nutrient and energy flow in tropical forests is certainly underappreciated.

Finally, there are snakes which prey partially or exclusively on other snakes. The elapids (cobras and kraits) are primarily snake-eaters, and the king cobra, *Ophiophagus hannah*, will eat nothing else.

Stephen Von Peltz

The King Cobra (*Ophiophagus hannah*) feeds exclusively on other snakes.

20

The rate of digestion in snakes, which are ectotherms, depends on their ability to seek suitable environmental temperatures. Most sea snakes remain in the ocean and thus are at the mercy of the temperature of the aquatic habitat. Sea kraits of the Laticaudinae, however, come ashore almost immediately after feeding, probably to take advantage of the elevated temperatures available on land. Like many tropical land snakes, they seem to prefer a body temperature of about 31°C; digestion is probably more efficient than the sea temperatures which can be as low as 26°C. during certain seasons. *Laticauda colubrina* is extremely adept at seeking out microenvironments of suitable temperature, even though temperatures on their rocky islets can range from a low of about 26°C. near the water's edge, to above 45°C. (well above the 36–38°C. lethal temperature) in areas of direct sun. The preferred body temperature for most snakes in Borneo is probably between 29–31°Celsius. Montane species may be active at slightly lower temperatures, however.

Since snakes do depend on environmental heating, they tend to digest their food over several days or weeks (unlike the hours or even minutes characteristic of mammals and birds), and so do not feed very frequently. The metabolic rate of a snake is, in fact, less than one-tenth of that for a similarly-sized mammal. Thus, most snakes tend to seek shelter after a meal and sleep, or at least rest while the digestion process is completed. Tropical vipers such as *Trimeresurus* are remarkably "lazy", sleeping away most of their days, and waking up only to strike at a passing prey animal once every few weeks. They probably move very little throughout their entire lives. Other species such as cat-snakes, racers or cobras are much more active, covering considerably more territory. Nevertheless, following a meal they too will tend to seek shelter for a few days to ensure uninterrupted digestion. Snakes which have recently fed will often regurgitate a meal (as well as evacuate their cloaca), if roughly handled—to the dismay of many a herpetologist, amateur or professional.

Although we have scientific data on diets and capture locations for a number of Bornean snake species, the life histories of most remain relatively unknown. Studies of the ecology of particular species inevitably turn up interesting details. The sea krait *Laticauda colubrina* for example, was known to be common, but the extent of its distribution was not well documented. Now it is obvious that it is one of Borneo's most common snakes, frequenting almost any waterless, rocky island near coral reefs in shallow coastal seas. Differences in the growth rates and habits of the sexes of the sea kraits have also been worked out. Males are much smaller than females, usually less than one metre in total length. However, they reach adult length much sooner than the opposite sex, and spend most of their time ashore on rocky islets, seeking to mate with arriving females. The latter on the other hand, grow rapidly for more than twice the duration of male growth, attaining a total length of almost two metres after about ten years. However, unlike the males they must spend most of their time at sea, feeding. The result is a sex ratio on some islands greatly in favor of males, up to five to one. Young females apparently suffer high mortality because of the increased time spent foraging at sea. Interestingly, despite its great abundance in Borneo, the eggs of *Laticauda colubrina* have never been found.

For land snakes the information is even more sketchy, since finding enough individuals of most forest species for study is extremely difficult. We still know virtually nothing about densities, home ranges, social interactions, growth rates or longevity. Olfactory stimuli are probably the most important cues for snakes to locate one another, so that apparent "rarity" of some species may in fact be more the result of our inability to locate them (since we depend on our vision so completely).

R.B. Stuebing

A resting group of the Yellow-Lipped Sea Krait (*Laticauda colubrina*) from Pulau Keeraman, Sabah.

22

Sexual dimorphism is fairly common in Bornean snakes, and in virtually all species, the tail of the male is both thicker at the base, and longer in proportion to body length than that of the female. In some species such as sea kraits, females may be neary twice the length of males and three to four times heavier. In many other species, however, males and females are not so easily distinguished by size. Courtship and mating habits are incompletely known, though virtually all snakes possess similar basic courtship movements, such as "head jerking" by males. Territorial fighting may occur in pit-vipers (such as *Trimeresurus* spp.) and cobras (*Naja sumatrana*), though this is yet to be actually documented in Borneo. The bodies of all mating snakes become intertwined, and the male inserts one side of his bilobed (Y-shaped) hemipenes, and sperm enter the females cloaca along a special groove. Mating may take from several minutes to an hour or more. Females may not actually lay eggs immediately following copulation, but store the male's sperm for many months. Eggs must be laid in a stable microenvironment such as dead wood, leaf litter or a natural cavity where temperature is a constant 29–31°C. and humidity remains high, above 70%. Fluctuations in any of these conditions can easily cause egg mortality, developmental abnormalities or uneven sex ratios.

The oblong, leathery-shelled snake eggs hatch anywhere from as little as 45 days to as long as four months after they are laid, and hatchlings disperse quickly from the nest. For ovoviviparous snakes ("live" bearers that produce fully-formed young), apparently babies are not cared for in any way, but disperse quickly from the birthing site. Recent work on rattlesnakes (pit-vipers from the western United States) suggests however that some crotalids do stay with the hatchling snakes until the latter shed their skins for the first time. Clutch sizes for sea snakes (eggs or fully formed young) range from about 7–20, while the terrestrial pythons and colubrids can lay more than 40 eggs or give birth to dozens of young.

Growth is usually slow, and though few rates have actually been measured for land snakes in their natural habitat, studies on sea snakes (*Laticauda colubrina* and *Enhydrina schistosa*) indicate a rate of one to two millimetres per day is maintained at least through the first year. Most males grow more slowly than females, and reach their maximum size earlier, though exceptions exist (e.g., *Lapemis curtus*, in which the sexes are the same size).

Finally, although most people regard snakes as fierce predators (and they are important in the control of rodents, for example), they have numerous natural enemies. In the forest, wild pigs are said to be one of the most efficient snake predators, and are voracious feeders on small vertebrates. Many species of large predatory birds, from hawks to crow-pheasants commonly eat snakes. The Crested Serpent Eagle is named after its diet, and is often seen flying with a snake in its talons. Similarly, the White-Bellied Sea Eagle of coastal waters feeds heavily upon sea snakes of all kinds, apparently without harm. Most humans, of course, never hesitate to kill a snake, and pythons in particular are eaten by many of the peoples of Borneo.

In any case, snakes remain among the least understood and perhaps the least appreciated of the vertebrate animals of Borneo. What is their ecological importance to the forest? The little research that has been completed suggests that snakes play a major ecological role in the forest floor leaf litter community. Snakes may also be one of the most significant predators of the forest canopy. New perspectives are certain to be gained from further research.

Snake Conservation

Borneo covers an area of roughly 80% the size of Texas in the U.S.A.,
and though similar in size, is far richer in plant and animal species
than almost any other areas outside the tropics. The tremendous
variety of the Bornean topography and associated vegetation provides a vast
range of habitats for complex biological communities to occur.

Earlier in this century, Borneo was mostly covered by dense forests of
which about 50% exist today, mostly as secondary growth. Along the coast,
plant communities were associations of mangrove, peat swamp and *kerangas*
vegetation, giving way to lowland and mixed dipterocarp forests with
canopies from 30–60 m in height. Both plant and animal communities
changed rather abruptly around 1000 metres above sea level, where hill
dipterocarp forests relinquished their dominance to oak and other
submontane forests, and on some mountains (Kinabalu, Trus Madi, Mulu and
a few others) to gnarled montane and (Mount Kinabalu) alpine vegetation.

Wildlife conservation in Borneo is a phenomenon of the last 50 years,
since the island saw little serious disturbance to natural habitats until the late
1950s. In some inland areas, shifting cultivation by interior peoples modified
the species composition of the forest. Nevertheless, after a regeneration
period of about thirty years or so, differences with old growth forests would
not be immediately obvious to a non-taxonomist. By the 1970s, however,
conspicuous changes to the landscape were taking place from rapid
economic development and population growth in Indonesian and Malaysian
Borneo. In the 1990s, it has become clear that wildlife has been eliminated
over vast areas, and we have reached a critical juncture in the survival of
some animal species in Borneo.

Until recently, herpetofauna were left out of most conservation
strategies. Perhaps because so little was known about their distributions and
population dynamics that they were frequently overlooked. Changes are

25

underway, however, as reflected in the inclusion of herpetofaunal surveys within the management plans of protected areas in Borneo[6] and the listing of certain snake species under CITES (Convention on International Trade in Endangered Species).

One of the challenges facing conservationists arises because of the secretive nature of many snake species in Borneo. The status of species which are fossorial, e.g., live under leaf litter, soil, bark or moss is difficult to determine. Some genera, such as *Cylindrophis* or *Xenophidion*, have species that have been seen only once, though this may not in itself prove that they are rare or endangered. Ironically, the only species that have received protection under the law are the two species of pythons, which are presently rather common.

The known kinds of pressures on snake abundance in Borneo are of two types: human use and habitat destruction. Human exploitation includes the use of snakes as food and medicine, and the selling of snake products such as skins. Although it is undeniable that trade in snake products exists, it is yet to reach significant levels in Borneo, despite the opportunistic selling of snake meat locally to small restaurants. Trade in snake skins is also on a rather small scale, since it is in much less demand than, for example, crocodile skin. The species involved are almost exclusively pythons, though a few others such as the file snakes or even the sea kraits have been used for reptile leather.

A far more significant and serious threat to snake populations is the conversion of natural habitats for agricultural or industrial use. Changes of this type bring drastic alterations to the microclimate of the forest floor and canopy, where the majority of Borneo's more than one hundred terrestrial snakes are found. The problem lies in the highly specialized lifestyles of many species, in diet or in temperature and moisture requirements. The enormous changes that take place when forest is removed can quickly bring about the demise of species through dessication, lethal temperatures and loss of prey items. For example, the mountain reed snake, *Oreocalamis hanitschi*, has been found only at elevations of approximately 1200–1500 metres, in oak forests. Because most of the Bornean terrain lies below 1200 metres in altitude, these forests have never abundant, and are now disappearing rapidly since their cooler temperatures and relatively fertile soils offer excellent

---

[6] Bornean examples are the Lanjak-Entimau Wildlife Sanctuary (Sarawak, Malaysia) and the Bentuang-Karimun National Park (West Kalimantan, Indonesia).

prospects for agriculture, from vegetable farms to exotic tree plantations. While it is not known whether the mountain reed snake can survive in plantations or vegetable gardens, it is highly unlikely that it can survive the heat and dryness associated with the clearing of oak forest and the early stages, or planting phase, of the agricultural schemes.

A few decades ago, no one would have predicted that forest fires could become a major problem in Borneo. The relentless pace of development over the last thirty years, however, have created conditions far different from those which existed in the past. By the year 2000, the vast majority of Borneo's inland forests below 1000 metres elevation will have been logged at least once. The logging generally dries out the forest by opening the canopy, while producing considerable woody debris from the damage to trees not extracted. Peat swamp forests are frequently drained for eventual conversion to agriculture, yet another process by which remaining tree stands dry out significantly. In the absence of a human presence, perhaps these forests would regenerate, along with their herpetofauna, which studies have shown frequently survives and returns within a decade or two. However, many logged out areas are deemed suitable for plantation agriculture, and cleared by burning. Logging roads also provide access for settlers looking for suitable areas for slash and burn agriculture. As has been so clearly demonstrated by the severe burning and haze in Borneo during 1997–98, fire is a conservation problem not to be underestimated. A significant portion of the local snake fauna will not survive such an extreme environmental challenge, and will be slow indeed to recover, even if pockets of survivors do remain.

Because the majority of Bornean snakes are forest species, isolation of patches or "islands" of forest will undoubtedly have an effect on the genetics of snake populations, reducing their genetic diversity by the creation of barriers of unsuitable (= unaltered) habitats. Populations of a large number of forest species, particularly in the lowlands, but in some highland areas as well, are fragmented or isolated. The long term effect of this increasingly common situation is not known for sure, though some scientists predict localized extinction for species in which the genetic variability becomes severely reduced.

For intact habitats, however, we have as yet no real proof that snake populations are declining in Borneo. Realistically, however, there is not a single forest species on which population studies have been done, and for which we have any real idea what their actual status is. There are, in fact, few species of which enough individuals could be found within a reasonable length of time, to permit a meaningful study to be carried out. All we can say is that from fieldwork in forests over the past ten years or so, that certain species such as *Amphiesma flavifrons*, *Rhabdophis chrysarga*, *Calamaria* spp. and *Trimeresurus wagleri* are frequently encountered and have not declined as far as we know.

Marine snakes face serious challenges via the loss of coral reefs from siltation, the result of coastal development. The impact of reef loss via siltation, trawling, or fish bombing is unclear, but it is unlikely that specialists such as *Laticauda colubrina*, the Yellow-Lipped Sea Krait (which feeds on reef-living eels), can benefit from these changes. Recent studies by Anna Wong at the Sabah Museum have shown however that despite the tremendous mortality that occurs in several species of sea snakes (*Lapemis curtus, Hydrophis* spp.) from intensive trawling for prawns off the West coast of Sabah, these species remain amazingly abundant.

A third potential threat of which almost nothing is known is the accumulation of pesticide residues through the food chain, which can be substantial since all snakes are predators. The insidious feature of this threat is that many snake species could disappear even before much is known about them. Interestingly, the importance of small snake species in the forest in the dynamics of the leaf litter community, and thus the cycling of nutrients, has only just been recognized. In agricultural areas, snakes are potentially beneficial in the control of pests (such as cobras and racers, which consume rats in oil palm estates). However, we know little or nothing of the effects of agricultural chemicals, particularly those used against weeds and undergrowth, on these snake species. Since snakes are predators frequently at or near the top of the food chain, it can be expected that persistent pesticides will accumulate in their bodies. Again, the long term effects of these chemicals have not been studied.

Legislating snake conservation will essentially mean preserving intact natural habitats of sufficient quantity (area) and quality to ensure stability for physical and biotic habitats, especially of forest species. Among forest species, the most sensitive and easily lost are those of submontane and montane areas, whose distributions are patchy and whose habitats rapidly degrade with disturbance. Lowland areas are at least as important, since a larger proportion of species are present in these forests, and lowland forests are currently under the heaviest pressure for conversion to other forms of land use. It is undeniable, however that the species richness of the snake commun ity of a plantation is a mere fraction of that of even a secondary forest.

the Short, or Blood Python (*Python curtus*) is less well known, but this species also appears to be holding its own.

Snake blood and gall bladders are also in demand, particularly in Bornean cities, as treatment for poor eyesight and arthritis. The blood of the Sumatran Cobra (*Naja sumatrana*) is taken with Chinese wine by elderly people as a tonic. Cobras are probably not in any imminent danger of extinction, since they are common in disturbed areas. Reduction of their numbers is undesirable, however, since they help to control rats.

Snake bite

Cases of snake bite in Borneo are rarely reported, but probably uncommon. Interestingly, one of the most abundant snakes in urban areas is the Sumatran Cobra (*Naja sumatrana*). Both in villages and town areas, most bites by venomous snakes are attributable to cobras. Juvenile cobras, banded black and white, are sometimes handled by persons who assume that all dangerous snakes (e.g., cobras) are entirely black. Cobras in Sabah and Sarawak often turn up in houses, probably in search of rats. Just a few years ago, a 30 cm cobra was found in the store room of a major bank in Kuching.

Though few people will believe it, snakes almost never bite without provocation, and some tolerate a fair bit of disturbance before they defend themselves. In the 1980's, one of us (RBS) was accompanying a well-known American bird photographer through the Kota Kinabalu campus of the local university, when the photographer innocently reached into a shallow drain and picked up a snake. When told that it was a cobra, he released it, but not before lifting it some distance off the ground and peering at it intently. The snake hissed hesitantly, but spread its hood and raised its head only after hitting the ground. It never attempted to bite.

Once captured, this same snake did try to bite, and then sprayed venom in a fine mist for a distance of perhaps half a metre. This species is well known for this behaviour. A local physician in Kota Kinabalu once sent a snake to the university for identification after it had sprayed venom into the left eye of a nine-year old boy. The eye was not damaged, and required only saline eye drops as treatment. After some localised irritation and redness, there were no further complications.

Snake bites do cause panic and people rush to treat the victim in any way possible. Sometimes, however, the "treatment" of a bite is more damaging than the bite itself. This certainly applies in cases where a villager cuts off a finger after a snake bite assumed to be venomous. Near Kuching, Sarawak, some years ago, a woman was bitten by an unidentified snake. A tight tourniquet was applied, and traditional herbs used to treat the wound. The woman recovered, but her hand was permanently affected. Since there were no other symptoms following the bite, it is likely that most of the damage was done by the tourniquet.

Admittedly, bites of venomous species, particularly cobras, can be extremely dangerous. Dr Neville Haile (author of a well-known key to Bornean snakes), writes of a Dusun youth from Kinarut in Sabah who encountered a three-metre king cobra (*Ophiophagus hannah*) and attacked it with a stick. Breaking the snake's back, he assumed it dead, but when he kicked the head, he was bitten on the foot. Killing the snake, he hurried back to his village, where he succumbed within two hours. The *Borneo News* of 23 December, 1958 reported that after the man died, the village people "skinned the snake and ate the flesh"[8]. Interestingly, despite the King Cobra's reputation for aggressiveness, the snake struck only in defense. As for the behaviour of the victim, rushing back to his village he undoubtedly facilitated the spread of the venom, and his rapid demise. Finally, the villagers' eating the snake may not have been exclusively for purposes of revenge, since large snakes are considered delicacies in Sabah to this day.

Elapid venoms, when vigourously circulated through the body, paralyse the heart and diaphragm, and death comes swiftly. Peter S. Lloyd, a plantation manager from the Membakut area of Sabah was bitten on April 27, 1958 by a banded krait (*Bungarus fasciatus*), a nocturnal member of the cobra family. His tombstone (opposite page) lies at the base of Signal Hill in Kota Kinabalu, with the simple epitaph, "Died of snake bite". The Banded Krait is certainly dangerous, and should be treated with the utmost caution. In Borneo, at least, this krait is more aggressive than its behaviour as described in Tweedie[9].

Dr Peter Ashton, one of Borneo's foremost forest botanists, was bitten by a viper (reputedly *Ovophis chaseni*, but possibly *Trimeresurus borneensis*) in February, 1959 while on fieldwork near ulu Belalong, Brunei. His symptoms were acute pain and swelling, which worsened over two days until he had to

---

[8] Haile, N.S. 1958. The Snakes of Borneo, with a key to the species. *Sarawak Museum Journal* 8: 743–771.
[9] Tweedie, M.W.F. 1983. *Snakes of Malaya* (3rd Edition).

R.B. Stuebing

Tombstone of of Peter S. Lloyd in Kota Kinabalu, Sabah.

be carried out by his Iban workers. He arrived at the Brunei State Hospital and despite his initially good condition, collapsed the following day with severe internal bleeding. After treatment, which included blood transfusions, he recovered gradually over a period of several weeks.

These stories illustrate the potential seriousness of snake bite cases especially in the field. It should be emphasised however, that snake bite is not only a rare occurrence, but also rarely fatal. One reason is that a substantial number of bites, up to one-third of all cases, are apparently "dry", with no venom injected. Two families (Elapidae and Crotalidae) can however deliver potentially fatal bites. Several "rear-fanged" species (Colubridae) are known to have a weak venom which is not regarded as dangerous to humans, though some natricine snakes should be treated with caution[10]. Again, families which should regarded as particularly dangerous are the Elapidae, which includes the sea snakes, cobras, kraits and coral snakes, and the Crotalidae, which consists of the vipers.

Bites from cobras are not initially painful, but cause progressive numbness, paralysis of the skeletal muscles (reflected in droopy eyelids of the victims) and eventually paralysis of the diaphragm and heart. Cobra venom can also cause permanent crippling of hands or feet. A colleague who assisted in our collecting of sea snake specimens for the local university showed me two crooked fingers on one hand, the result of a cobra bite when he was young.

The most toxic venoms are found in the sea snakes (Hydrophiinae), which are routinely plucked from prawn trawls by fishermen, who then pitch them back overboard. One day at the Kota Kinabalu port, about a dozen live research specimens were purchased from a local fisherman, who had collected them live from his trawler. Since he was being paid for each snake, he reached into his bucket and lifted out the writhing creatures one by one, dropping them into a bucket with an loud, "One, Two, Three..." When he reached the bottom of his pail, having calmly handled some of the most deadly creatures on earth, he pointed into his container and said in Malay:

---

[10] A group of colubrid water snakes in Borneo, the Homalopsinae, are rear fanged and the venom have caused localised pain and swelling, but no reported cases in Borneo have ever required special treatment. Some other snakes, such as *Ahaetulla prasina* or the cat snakes (*Boiga* spp.) are known to be rear-fanged and venomous, but no symptoms in humans have ever been reported. The first author has been bitten numerous times by *Boiga dendrophila* without symptoms beyond profuse bleeding (from puncture wounds inflicted by long teeth).

"You get that one. That one is *jahat* ("bad news"). We peered over to see what could possibly be worse than what he had just handled, and he pointed to a live file snake (*Acrochordus granulatus*), the only non-venomous snake of the lot. The snake was lifted out barehanded with great fanfare, much to the fisherman's awe and astonishment. Telling him that it was harmless did not seem to diminish the accomplishment.

Snake bite treatment[11]

There are many sources of information for treatment of snake bite, the most current of which are available on the Internet, under "snakebite". Bites are rare, and the majority of cases are by non-venomous species. An incident can frequently be avoided by exercising reasonable caution. Look before placing hands or feet either on the ground, on old logs or stumps or near low vegetation such as rattan clumps. If you encounter a snake, do not approach or disturb it, but retreat slowly. Fast movements will cause some snakes to become alarmed, and their path of retreat may be in your direction. If so, step aside! The following recommendations on the treatment are merely a summary, and intended only to provide basic information.

DO

1. Remain calm and avoid moving unless you are alone and need to seek help.
2. Allow the bite to bleed freely for 30 seconds.
3. If a first-aid kit is available, cleanse and disinfect the site of the bite.
4. Press a gauze pad (preferably soaked in Betadine or antiseptic solution) over the bite, and strap firmly with adhesive tape.
5. Wrap an elastic bandage, or clean cloth **firmly** (but not so tight as to cut off circulation) in both directions from the site of the bite (if the bite is on an arm/hand or leg/foot).
6. Immobilise a bitten extremity with a splint.
7. Keep the bite below the heart or in a "gravity dependent" position below the body.

---

[11] Most of this information has been taken from an internet posting by S. Grenard in 1996, and incorporates a wide range of opinion on the best approach and treatment for snakebite. There are severl such sites on the Internet, which are updated regularly.

8. Go to the nearest hospital or medical facility as soon as possible
9. If the snake has been killed, bring it for identification (kill it only if it is safe to do so!)

DON'T

1. Run or move strenuously.
2. Remove any pressure bandage until you reach a hospital. As soon as the dressing is released, venom will spread, so that intensive emergency treatment must be at hand.
3. Eat or drink (unless permitted by medical personnel).
4. Cut or incise bite.
5. Drink alcohol or use oral medication.
6. Apply hot or cold packs.
7. Apply narrow, tight tourniquets such as cords or belts.
8. Waste time for **any** reason in seeking medical assistance.

Snake bite kits should contain at least one roll each of 5 cm and 8 cm ACE or comparable elastic bandages with clips (the kind used for joint support, such as sprains); several 10×10 cm sterile gauze pads; a small bottle of betadine solution; one roll each of 1.5 cm and 3 cm surgical tape.

The best policy for non-herpetologists, of course, is to avoid contact with snakes and not to disturb them.

A Key to the Snakes of Borneo

1   Tail flat, oar-shaped; marine snakes 89
     Tail round, tapered; land or freshwater snakes 2

2   Eyes hidden by head scales .... Typhlopidae (p. 57)
     Eyes not hidden by head scales 3

3   Tail extremely short, stout, and sharply pointed 4
     Tail not as above 5

4   Underside of head with median or "mental" groove (Fig. 1C) ....
     .... *Cylindrophis* sp.[12] (p. 60)
     Underside of head without median groove .... *Anomochilus* spp. (p. 63)

5   Sensory pits present on side of head or on labial scales (Fig. 3A, B) 6
     No such pits 13

6   A single sensory pit located between the eye and nostril 7
     Sensory pits on lips 12

7   Sides of head marked with a dark band or stripe 8
     No such band or stripe 10

8   Reddish brown stripe running along upper edge of the snout; sides of
     head whitish or yellowish .... *Tropidolaemus wagleri* (p. 233)
     No stripe on snout; stripe behind or below eye 9

---

[12] The most commonly encountered species is *Cylindrophis ruffus*, though many other, rarer species exist.

9   Diagonal white-edged stripe or band from behind eye to corner of mouth
.... *Ovophis chaseni* (p. 223)
Indistinct dark, stripe diagonally behind eye to corner of mouth; con-
spicuously protruding nasal scale ..... *Trimeresurus borneensis* (p. 225)

10   All body scales with light green tip and black base, giving the
appearance of green scales edged in black ....
....*Trimeresurus malcolmi* (p. 227)
Greenish, but not as above 11

11   Sides of head greenish; white line along lower part of body ....
.... *Trimeresurus popeorum* (p. 229)
Sides of head yellowish white, body frequently with dark indistinct
bands or markings .... *Trimeresurus sumatranus* (p. 231)

12   Sensory pits on only two upper labial scales; body short and thick ....
.... *Python curtus* (p. 65)
Sensory pits on four upper labial scales; body more slender, not short and
thick .... *Python reticulatus* (p. 67)

13   Top of snout with a pair of very large scales; all head scales much
smaller (Fig. 4A) .... *Xenophidion acanthognathus* (p. 71)
Scales on top of snout not as above 14

14   Interparietal scale as large as parietal (Fig. 4B) ....
.... *Xenopeltis unicolor* (p. 69)
No interparietal scale 15

15   Snout squarish and blunt; each scale with a hard, bony bump making the
texture of the skin like coarse sandpaper 16
Snout not as above, skin scales otherwise (Fig. 2B, C) 17

16   Body blackish with light grey bands; marine snake ....
.... *Acrochordus granulatus* (p. 73)
Body greenish or yellowish brown; river snake ....
.... *Acrochordus javanicus* (p. 74)

17   A straight transverse row of small scales across the snout immediately in
front of the eyes (Fig. 4C) .... *Stoliczkaia borneensis* (p. 77)

Head scales not as above 18

18 Rough, tiny scales covering the entire top portion of the head except for
    two oval, bony plates at the nostrils (Fig. 4D) ....
    .... *Xenodermus javanicus* (p. 81)
    Head scales not as above 19

19 With no midline groove under chin (Fig. 1D) 20
    With midline groove under chin (Fig. 1C) 23

20 Head larger than neck, diameter of eye larger than its distance to the
    nostril; subcaudal scales in a single row .... *Aplopeltura boa* (p. 83)
    Eye smaller, head not larger than neck; subcaudal scales paired 21

21 Head and neck dark brown, much darker than body ....
    .... *Pareas malaccanus* (p. 88)
    Head and neck not as above 22

22 Dark x-shaped marking on back of neck .... *Pareas nuchalis* (p. 89)
    No such marking, except for scattered dark bars on sides of neck ....
    .... *Pareas laevis* (p. 86)

23 Nostrils on top of head; water snakes 24
    Nostrils on sides of snout 31

24 Lower jaw much shorter than upper jaw ...... *Fordonia leucobalia* (p. 95)
    Lower jaw not as above 25

25 Top of head behind eyes covered with small scales ....
    .... *Cerberus rynchops* (p. 91)
    Top of head behind eyes with large scales or shields 26

26 Body with dark-edged light crossbars that do not extend across the belly
    .... *Homalopsis buccata* (p. 96)
    Body not marked as above 27

27 Body striped .... *Enhydris enhydris* (p. 94)
    Body not striped 28

28 Narrow light crossband behind head .... *Enhydris punctata* (p. 95)
    No light cross band behind head 29

29 Both upper body and underside with dark crossbars ....
    .... *Enhydris alternans* (p. 95)
    Body not marked as above 30

30 Belly orangish or yellowish with large scattered black blotches ....
    .... *Enhydris doriae* (p. 94)
    Ventrals light orangish to pinkish with narrow dark edges ....
    .... *Enhydris plumbea* (p. 93)

31 Prefrontal scales and internasal scales fused (Fig. 4E) ....
    .... *Calamaria* spp. (p. 127)
    Prefrontal scales and internasal scales not as above 32

32 Pupil elongated horizontally (Fig. 5B) 33
    Pupil not elongated horizontally 35

33 Body green .... *Ahaetulla prasina* (p. 114)
    Body not green 34

34 Snout sharply pointed, eyes protruding .... *Ahaetulla fasciolata* (p. 114)
    Snout tapered but not sharp, eyes not protruding ....
    .... *Dryophiops rubescens* (p. 144)

35 Pupil elongated vertically (Fig. 5C) 36
    Pupil round (Fig. 5A) 49

36 Scales smooth (Fig. 2B) 37
    Scales keeled (Fig. 2C) 47

37 Head at least twice as wide as neck 38
    Head not twice as wide as neck 42

38 Body black with bright yellow bands .... *Boiga dendrophila* (p. 120)
    Body not as above 39

39 Body greenish or greenish grey .... *Boiga drapiezii* (p. 122)

Body yellowish or brown 40

40 Throat yellowish, body tan to dark brown with dark markings ....
.... *Boiga cynodon* (p. 118)
Body not as above 41

41 Dark spotted pattern on top of head .... *Boiga jaspidea* (p. 124)
No spots on head .... *Boiga nigriceps* (p. 126)

42 Head slightly wider than neck, top and sides of snout (in front of eye)
form a sharp angle or edge; small snakes 43
Head not as above 47

43 Symmetrical pattern of dark streaks on top of head (Fig. 7B) ....
.... *Psammodynastes pulverulentus* (p. 112)
No pattern of dark streaks; nape dark with light patch (Fig. 7A) ....
.... *Psammodynastes pictus* (p. 110)

44 Body yellowish brown with three distinct light stripes ....
.... *Dryocalamus tristrigatus* (p. 142)
Body not as above 45

45 Body light brown with a series of dark brown patches across the back,
not reaching the ventrals .... *Dryocalamus subannulatus* (p. 144)
Body not so marked 46

46 Body dark brown to black marked with a light yellowish network; loreal
scale present .... *Lycodon aulicus* (p. 99)
Body brown, sometimes with pale yellow bands; loreal scale absent
.... *Lycodon effraenis* (p. 100)

47 Scales strongly keeled; keels with rough, serrated edges ....
.... *Lepturophis borneensis* (p. 96)
Scales weakly keeled 48

48 Upper part of body entirely dark with no pattern, snout rounded ....
.... *Stegonotus borneensis* (p. 164)
Body dark with white collar or white encircling bands ....
.... *Lycodon subcinctus* (p. 101)

49 Scales smooth 50
    Scales keeled 80

50 Ventral scales with a sharp angle or corner near outer edge (Fig. 6A, B)
    51
    Ventral scales not as above 60

51 An orange or yellow marking across the head between the eyes 52
    No such marking 53

52 Body with black and yellow banding .... *Chrysopelea pelias* (p. 135)
    Body speckled yellow and red, sides of body black ....
    .... *Chrysopelea paradisi* (p. 134)

53 Body partially or completely green 54
    Body not green 55

54 Body bright green[13], with red or grey tail ....
    .... *Gonyosoma oxycephalum* (p. 152)
    Body green, black and yellow, with diagonal orange bands in the
    posterior half .... *Gonyophis margaritatus* (p. 150)

55 Tail red .... *Elaphe erythrura* (p. 147)
    Tail not red 56

56 Dark band through the eye 57
    No dark band through eye .... *Dendrelaphis caudolineatus* (p. 136)

57 Vertebral scales larger than adjacent scales (Fig. 2A) 58
    Vertebral scales the same size as adjacent scales 59

58 Eye as large or larger in diameter than its distance from nostril ....
    .... *Dendrelaphis formosus* (p. 139)
    Eye less in diameter than its distance to the nostril ....
    .... *Dendrelaphis pictus* (p. 140)

---

[13] Some Sabah specimens are greyish with scales edged in black.

59 A single dark diagonal streak from behind eye towards the angle of the jaw; top of head unmarked .... *Elaphe flavolineata* (p. 146)
Two streaks running from behind the eye; a black cross band on the back of the head .... *Elaphe radiata* (p. 147)

60 Head with dark marking through eyes and over top of snout ....
.... *Oligodon* (p. 103)
Head not as above 61

61 Eye completely or partially separated from the upper labial scales by a row of small scales below the eye 62
Eye not as above 64

62 Body dark olive green to brown, with inverted, dark V-shaped markings on sides of neck; large snakes .... *Xenelaphis hexagonotus* (p. 80)
Body not as above; small snakes 63

63 Body light brown, unmarked .... *Hydrablabes periops* (p. 171)
Body dark brown, with an indistinct light line down the back and a light stripe along the sides .... *Hydrablabes praefrontalis* (p. 172)

64 Upper lip with dark-edged white streak ....
.... *Sibynophis melanocephalus* (p. 163)
Not as above 65

65 Tail short (less than 50 subcaudal scales) 66
Tail longer (more than 50 subcaudal scales) 69

66 Dark band through eye extending onto side of body ....
.... *Oreocalamus hanitschi* (p. 178)
Not as above 67

67 Body greyish black with a broad, complete yellowish-white to orange band on nape .... *Pseudorabdion albonuchalis* (p. 159)
Band absent 68

68 Two narrow, incomplete yellow rings behind head ....
.... *Pseudorabdion saravacensis* (p. 161)

Pattern not as above .... *Pseudorabdion longiceps* (p. 161)

.... *Pseudorabdion collaris* [14] (p. 161)

69 No loreal scale; third upper labial enlarged, touching eye and nasal scale (Fig. 4F) 70

Loreal scale present 75

70 Body bluish-black with light stripes; tail red 71

Coloration not as above 72

71 Head bright red-orange .... *Maticora bivirgata* (p. 193)

Head yellowish brown .... *Bungarus flaviceps* (p. 191)

72 Body with red stripe along back, belly black and white ....

.... *Maticora intestinalis* (p. 195)

Body not as above 73

73 Body with broad white (or yellowish) and black bands ....

.... *Bungarus fasciatus* [15] (p. 189)

Body not as above 74

74 Dorsal body all black, without pattern .... *Naja sumatrana* [16] (p. 197)

Body dark olive green to brown, without pattern ....

.... *Ophiophagus hannah* (p. 199)

75 A black or dark brown stripe down centre of back flanked by a reddish stripe on each side .... *Sibyophis geminatus* (p. 162)

Coloration otherwise 76

76 A dark-edged, white V-shaped marking on the nape ....

.... *Liopeltis longicauda* (p. 156)

---

[14] With a good hand lens, the preocular scale of *Pseudorabdion longiceps* can be seen. *P. collaris* lacks this scale.

[15] Juvenile cobras (*Naja sumatrana* and *Ophiophagus hannah*) also have yellowish cross-bands, as do juvenile wolf snakes (*Lycodon aulicus* and *L. subcinctus*).

[16] Juvenile *Naja sumatrana* have broad dirty white to yellowish cross bands on the body. Juvenile *Ophiophagus hannah* have narrow, yellowish cross bands on the body and head.

No light V on nape 77

77 A row of white spots down the back, starting at the neck ....
.... *Liopeltis baliodeirus* (p. 154)
Coloration otherwise 78

78 Dark stripe on side of head through eye, ending just behind neck; small
snake .... *Liopeltis tricolor* (p. 158)
Large snakes with different pattern 79

79 Tail and rear of body brown; scales edged with black ...... *Ptyas korros* [17]
Tail with sharply defined stripes on the sides .... *Zaocys fuscus* (p. 166)

80 Scales of head and body coarsely keeled; a ring of small scales between
eye and labials; labials subdivided horizontally ....
.... *Opisthotropis typica* (p. 176)
Scales not as above 81

81 Orange or reddish coloration on neck, contrasting with body 82
Coloration not as above 84

82 Sides of neck with triangular orange patches ....
.... *Xenochrophis trianguligera* (p. 187)
Not as above 83

83 Light V-shaped marking on nape, head brown ....
.... *Rhabdophis chrysarga* (p. 180)
No such marking; head black or dark grey ....
.... *Macropisthodon flaviceps* (p. 172)

84 White coloration on throat extending onto sides of neck, forming an
incomplete collar .... *Rhabdophis conspicillata* (p. 182)
Coloration not as above 85

85 A dark stripe down the back 86
No such stripe 87

---

[17] This species is a questionable record for Borneo, since it has not been recorded for about a hundred years.

86 Stripe narrow, beginning as a triangular-shaped mark on the nape ....
.... *Macropisthodon rhodomelas* (p. 175)
Stripe broad, belly light yellow bordered with black ....
.... *Xenochrophis maculata* (p. 185)

87 Head dark with conspicuous white spot on the snout ....
.... *Amphiesma flavifrons* (p. 168)
No white spot on the snout 88

88 Ventral scales with distinct black and white checkered pattern ....
.... *Amphiesma sarawacensis* (p. 170)
Ventrals not as above .... *Rhabdophis murudensis* (p. 184)

89 Distinct, enlarged ventral scales, about three to four times wider than
body scales 90
Scales in mid-line of belly less than three times width of adjacent scales
.... 91

90 Head dark brown or black, unicolored .... *Aipysurus eydouxii* (p. 205)
Top of snout white or yellow, top of head black ....
.... *Laticauda colubrina* (p. 202)

91 Head and fore part of body less than one-fourth of maximum body
diameter 92
Head and fore part of body more than one-third maximum diameter of
body 95

92 Head and neck dark without pale band behind head ....
.... *Microcephalophis gracilis* (p. 218)
Light band behind head on neck 93

93 Two postocular scales; keels on mid-body scales occupy full length of
scales .... *Hydrophis caerulescens* (p. 208)
One postocular scale; keels various 94

94 Keels occupy almost full length of scales; light bands of body bluish
grey .... *Hydrophis klossi* (p. 210)
Scales smooth or keels occupy less than half of scale length; light bands
of body yellowish white .... *Hydrophis fasciatus* (p. 208)

95 Tip of upper lip V-shaped and turned down over tip of lower jaw ....
.... *Enhydrina schistosa* (p. 206)
Tip of upper lip otherwise 96

96 Black above and lighter (yellow or white) below, with a sharp boundary
.... 97
Pattern with vertical banding 98

97 End of tail spotted .... *Pelamis platurus* (p. 219)
End of tail not spotted .... *Praescutata viperina* (p. 220)

98 Mid-body scale rows less than 25; dorsal body scales strongly keeled .....
.... *Kerilia jerdoni* (p. 214)
Mid-body scale rows more than 25; body scales smooth or not strongly
keeled 99

99 Eye separated from upper labials .... *Hydrophis ornatus* (p. 212)
One or two labials touch the eye 100

100 A pair of scales lying between the nasals and prefrontals ....
.... *Kolpophis annadalei* (p. 221)
Prefrontals meet nasals 101

101 A pair of narrow scales separating the nasals ....
.... *Thalassophis anomalus* (p. 222)
Nasals meet in midline 102

102 Dark bands completely encircle mid-body 103
Dark bands not encircling mid-body .... *Lapemis curtus* (p. 215)

103 Black bands much narrower near the belly than on the back ....
.... *Leioselasma cyanocincta*[18] (p. 216)
Black bands not tapered from back to belly 104

104 Light bands bluish grey or upper portion of body ....
.... *Hydrophis melanosoma* (p. 211)
Light bands dirty white to yellowish white .... *Hydrophis brookii* (p. 207)

---

[18] Only an experienced herpetologist can differentiate this species from *L. spiralis* (p. 217).

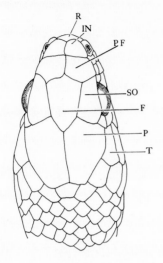

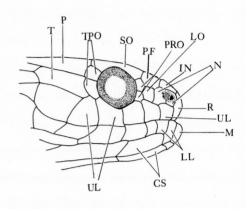

A. *Liopeltis baliodeirus*. Head, top view.   B. *Liopeltis baliodeirus*. Head, side view.

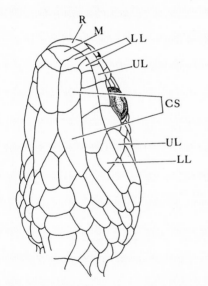

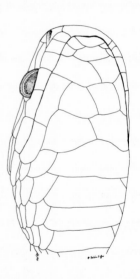

C. *Liopeltis baliodeirus*. Head, underside.   D. *Pareas laevis*. Head, underside.

Fig. 1. General head scalation. R= rostral, IN= internasal, PF= prefrontal, SO= supraocular, F= frontal, p= parietal, T= temporal, M= mental, CS= chin shields, UL= upper labials (= supralabials), LL= lower labials (=infralabials), TPO= postocular, PRO= preocular, LO= loreal, N= nasal

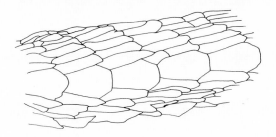

A. Enlarged vertebral row.

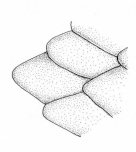

B. Smooth scales.

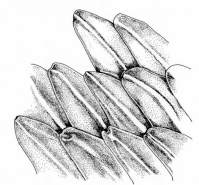

C. Keeled scales.

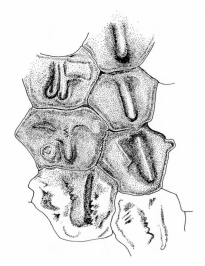

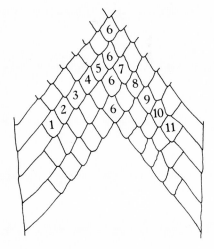

D. Blunt or knobby scales.   E. System for the numbering of scale rows.

Fig. 2. Scale shapes and patterns in Bornean snakes.

51

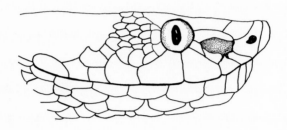

A. *Trimeresurus sumatratus.*

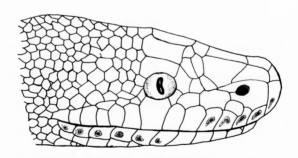

B. *Python reticulatus.*

Fig. 3. Sensory pits.

52

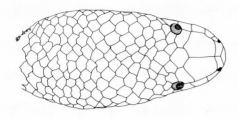

A. *Xenophidion acanthognathus.*

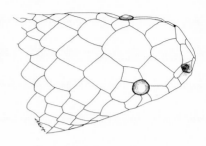

B. *Xenopeltis unicolor.*

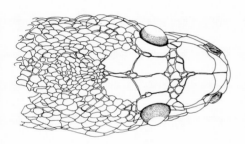

C. *Stoliczkaia borneensis.*

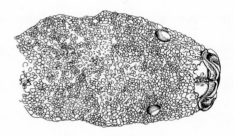

D. *Xenodermus javanicus.*

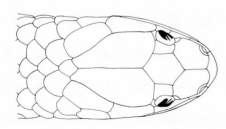

E. *Calamaria lumbricoidea.*

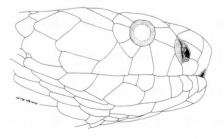

F. *Naja sumatrana.*

Fig. 4. Patterns of head scales.

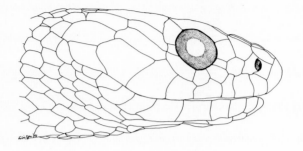

A. *Xenelaphis hexagonotus.*

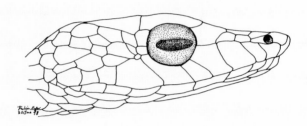

B. *Ahaetulla prasina.*

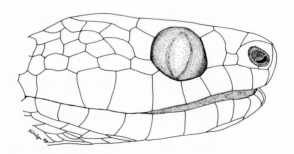

C. *Boiga dendrophila.*

Fig. 5. Pupil shapes and head scalation.

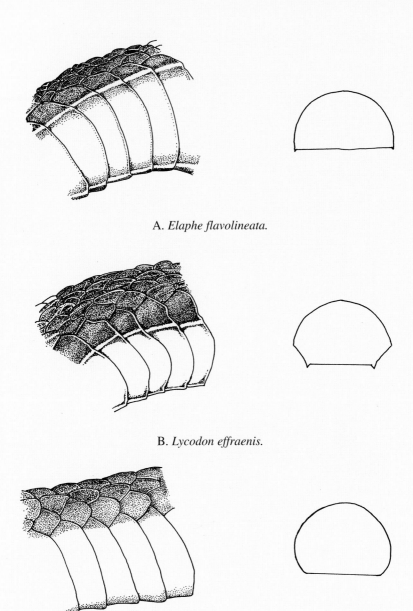

A. *Elaphe flavolineata.*

B. *Lycodon effraenis.*

C. *Liopeltis baliodeirus.*

Fig. 6. Types of ventral scale shapes and body shapes.

55

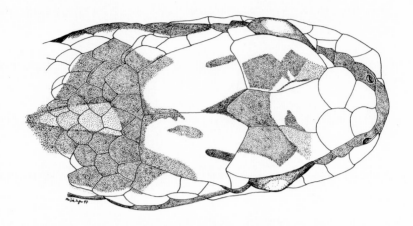

A. *Psammodynastes pictus.*

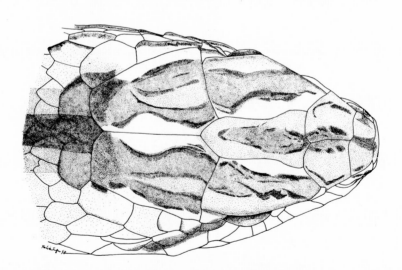

B. *Psammodynastes pulverulentus.*

Fig. 7. Head of mock vipers.

Typhlopidae, Cylindrophiidae and Anomochilidae
Blind Snakes and Pipe Snakes

Typhlopidae

Ramphotyphlops, Typhlops
Blind Snakes

Typhlops = blind. *Rhamphos* = a curving beak or bill, may refer to the sharp keel on the snout of a species known to early herpetologist.

We group these two genera of small, blind snakes because they are easy to recognize as a group but difficult to identify to species without a microscope and without access to a science library. They are small, usually less than 25 cm, smooth, rather hard, slender, and usually shiny. Their eyes are very small and covered by head shields. In some species, the eye is so small as to be almost invisible. These snakes are parallel-bodied; the head is as wide as the body, while the tail is always short and usually ends in a sharp spine. The scales of all rows are about the same size, so that distinctly widened ventral scales typical of the vast majority of snakes are absent. There is very little detailed information on the habitat and ecology of these species. All of them are burrowers and feed on ants or termites. Except for the common Flower Pot Snake, *Ramphotyphlops braminus*, they are rarely encountered.

57

Ramphotyphlops braminus
Common Blind Snake, Flower Pot Snake

Although described at the beginning of the nineteenth century from India, this species has turned up in all parts of the tropics and subtropics. It is the only snake in Borneo with a global distribution. The word *braminus* is likely to be derived from Hindi, since the first snakes of this genus were described from India.

This species is a slender, small snake with a maximum length of less than 20 cm. The eye, though very small and covered with head scales, is distinct. The snout is broadly rounded and the nostril points obliquely forward and to the side. There are 20 rows of scales around the body. The body is dark grey or dark brown, without a pattern, and somewhat lighter on the underside. The head is coloured like the body.

The common name of this species reflects habitat information and suggests an explanation for the global distribution. It lives in gardens and plantations feeding on ant larvae and pupae, and has undoubtedly been transported unknowingly through commerce secreted among the roots of plants. Common blind snakes are often washed onto walkways and into shallow drains by heavy rain. The species apparently does not occur in native forests.

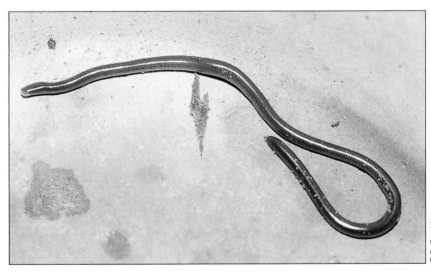

R.B. Stuebing

Ramphotyphlops braminus.

Ramphotyphlops lineatus
Striped Blind Snake

Originally described from Java, this species is now known also from southern Thailand, Peninsular Malaysia, Borneo, and Sumatra. The specific name is derived from *linea*, Latin, meaning line, referring to the pattern.

Although small, *Ramphotyphlops lineatus* is one of the large species in the group, reaching almost 50 cm. The snout is broadly rounded and the nostrils point downwards. The eye is extremely small and barely visible as a dark dot under the head scales. There are 22 rows of scales around the body.

In this distinctly marked species, each body scale has a yellow central area and dark edges that form 13 narrow dark lines separated by rows of alternating yellow and light brown spots. The underside is uniformly yellow. The head is mostly yellow, with brown scales behind the level of the tiny eyes.

Ramphotyphlops olivaceus
Keel-Nosed Blind Snake

Originally described from the Philippines, this species has also been reported from Borneo and the Sangihe Islands, south of the Philippines.

It reaches a maximum length of about 40 cm. The snout is broadly rounded but has a sharp, hard horizontal keel. The nostrils point downwards, while the small eye is distinct under the head scales. There are 20–22 scale rows around the body. The general colour is pale brown above and yellowish below. Each scale on the sides and top of the body has a brown centre and yellow edges, forming a series of narrow brown lines. The underside has similar, though much fainter lines.

A similar species, *Ramphotyphlops lorenzi*, was described from Pulau Miang Besar off the east coast of Borneo. It is like *R. olivaceus* in having a horizontal keel around the snout and with much the same coloration. Differences between these two species involve minor scale characters that may merely represent individual variation within a single species.

Typhlops muelleri
Bicolored Blind Snake

This species was originally described from Padang, West Sumatra, and is now known from Peninsular Malaysia and Borneo as well. It is named after a collector active in the Indo-Australian Archipelago in the early part of the nineteenth century.

Typhlops muelleri is a stout-bodied species reaching a maximum length of around 45 cm. The snout is broadly rounded and the nostrils point downwards. The eyes are distinct but covered by head scales. The body has 26 scale rows. The snakes are dark brown or black above, yellow below, the two colours sharply divided. The end of the body may have a broad yellow ring. The rim of the snout and sides of the head are yellow.

Typhlops koekoeki, a species described from a small island off the east coast of Kalimantan, is similar to *T. muelleri* in many ways, but the one poorly preserved specimen was grey (in alcohol) and slightly more slender.

Cylindrophiidae

The cylindrophids, or pipe snakes, have distinctly "pipe-shaped bodies with blunt heads and short, pointed tails. The ventrals are the same width as the dorsal scale rows, and they have 19–21 scale rows, and a median or mental groove under the chin. There is a single widespread species (*Cylindrophis ruffus*) and two other species in Borneo in which only one or at most a few specimens exist. They are secretive, and only *C. ruffus* is common in collections.

Cylindrophis engkariensis
Engkari Pipe Snake

The type locality for this species is western Sarawak. There is only one specimen known so far. *Kylinder* = a roller , *ophis* = snake. The second name is derived from the collection locality, the Engkari River in Sarawak.

The single known specimen of this species is 48.5 cm long. The blunt head is not wider than the neck, and the eyes are very small. The head and body are covered with glossy, smooth scales, with 17 rows at mid-body, and the tail comes to a sharp point. The ventrals are not wider than the other body scales, and not easily distinguished. The tail is short, thick and comes to a sharp point. There are 234 ventrals, subcaudals (plus one terminal pointed scale), and 6 supralabials, the third touching the eye.

The head and body are black, and there is a short, light streak running backwards from the eye. A row of white dots extends down the body on either side of the midline of the back. The sides have an irregular, interrupted white pattern. The chin is mostly black, while the underside has alternating black and white cross-bands divided at the midline. The tail is black above and white with black mottling below, except for the tip.

This *Cylindrophis* occurs far inland, in leaf litter on the forest floor. It probably feeds on small snakes and caecilians (amphibians), like other members of the genus.

Cylindrophis engkariensis.

61

Cylindrophis ruffus
Common Pipe Snake

The type locality for this species is unknown, but it has been found in the lowlands throughout South-east Asia. *Rufus* = reddish; in the original description the specific name was erroneously spelled *"ruffus"*.

This species reaches a maximum length of almost one metre, though most specimens are less than 50 cm. The head is short and blunt and not wider than the neck, and the eyes very small. The head and body are covered with glossy, smooth scales, with 19–21 rows at mid-body. The tail is short, thick and comes to a sharp point. There are 201–222 ventrals, 5–6 subcaudals (plus one terminal pointed scale), and 6 supralabials. The head and body are black, and there is usually a light "collar" behind the head. The colours of these bands, as well as a series of light patches along the upper surface is

J. Omar

Cylindrophis ruffus.

62

often bright orange. The chin is covered with mostly black scales with light edges, while the underside has black cross bands from throat to tail. The tail's sharp tip is black and has an encircling light band.

This *Cylindrophis* is common in museum collections, and so seems to be frequently encountered in the leaf litter of low, wet areas, perhaps emerging after heavy rains. Its habits are mostly unknown, though Tweedie (1983) reports that stomach contents contained insect larvae. It is viviparous, producing from 6–10 live young.

A third species of this genus, *Cylindrophis lineatus*, has been reported from Borneo twice. It differs from *C. ruffus* and *C. engkariensis* in having a pair of red or yellow stripes.

Anomochilidae

The differences between this family and the Cylindrophiidae are mainly internal, except for the lack of a mental (chin) groove in *Anomochilus*. Members of this family, like those of the Cylindrophiidae, are secretive and rarely encountered above ground.

Anomochilus leonardi
Leonard's Pipe Snake

The type locality for this species is in Pahang, Peninsular Malaysia. In Borneo it is known from a single snake from Sabah reported in 1993. *Anomo*, probably from *anomalos* = unusual, *chilus* = lip, perhaps referring to the absence of a groove under the chin.

The blunt head is not wider than the neck and is actually a bit narrower than the tail, which is pointed. The eye is minute. All the scales are smooth and glossy and are in 19 rows at mid-body. The total length of the Sabah specimen is 39 cm, with the tail only one cm. Ventrals 252; subcaudals 7; upper labials 4. In preservative, this specimen was purplish brown with conspicuous circular or oval light (orange to yellowish in life) spots on the side and on the belly.

Almost nothing is known of the natural history of this species. The single known Bornean specimen was found in lowland rain forest. A female specimen from the mainland contained four eggs. Weber's Pipe Snake (*Anomochilus weberi*), a similar species having 19 (v. 17) posterior scale rows, and more than 240 mid-ventral scales, has been recorded from Kalimantan. The relationship between these two species needs further study.

Pythonidae, Xenopeltidae, Xenophidiidae and Acrochordiae
Pythons, Earth Snakes and File Snakes

Pythonidae

Pythons and boas used to be grouped under a single family (the Boidae) but have now been separated. In Borneo, there are only two species, *Python reticulatus* and *Python curtus*, both widespread in South-east Asia. These have broad muscular heads, a vertical pupil, heat-sensitive pits on the lips and a pair of small claws on either side of the anus. Female pythons in captivity have been observed to incubate their eggs by coiling around them and generating heat by tetanic muscular contraction. The generic name is a Greek word referring to the mythical serpent killed by the god Apollo.

Python curtus
Short or Blood Python

This species was first described from Sumatra, but it is widely distributed in lowland areas of South-east Asia. Although it has been reported from numerous localitites in Borneo at elevations below 1000 metres, it is much less frequently seen than the reticulate python. *Curtus* = short, referring to the body of this species, which attains considerable girth, but only a modest length.

The maximum total length for the short python is reported to be less than three metres, and most specimens rarely exceed two metres, with a tail length

(Above). *Python curtus,* Adult. (Below). Juvenile.

of about 10% of the total. The head is flattened slightly like other pythons, but small relative to the size of the body. The eye is also small, with a vertical pupil. Heat sensitive pits occur on the rostral scale, first and second upper labials and as a groove along the posterior lower labial scales behind and below the eye There are 53–57 smooth rows of scales. The ventrals are slightly narrower than in most other land snakes, and range from 160–175. There are 26–32 paired subcaudals. Upper labials range from 10–11. As in other pythons, there is a small pair of claws located at the anus. The top of the head is light brown to brown with a pattern of several dark streaks. The sides of the snout are similar in colour, and there is a white stripe running diagonally from behind the eye to the angle of the jaw and onto the underside of the neck. The side of the head is dark brown behind the white stripe. The chin is dirty white to cream. The body is tan to brown, and the shade and pattern are variable. There is frequently a series of long, dark irregular blotches separated initially by white spots, which gradually elongate to become an irregular white stripe down the dorsal part of the tail. The sides are light coloured with wavy dark elongated areas bordered in white. The ventrals are cream coloured with some indistinct dark mottling.

Short pythons are rather secretive, and found primarily in wet habitats including under the banks of streams both in forests and cultivated areas. They feed on small vertebrates, mostly rodents, and lay from 10–15 eggs. Despite their sluggish appearance, they can strike with amazing speed.

Python reticulatus
Reticulate Python

The type locality for this species is unknown, but it is widely distributed and common throughout South-east Asia. It is common in the lowlands of Borneo at elevations below 1000 metres. *Reticulatus* means netlike, from *rete* = net, referring to the netlike markings on the body.

This species holds the record as the longest snake in the world, having a documented total length of up to 10 metres, though such individuals are now extremely rare in Borneo. The tail is about 12–15% of total length. The head is flattened slightly and almost guitar-shaped, while other notable features are the vertical pupil of the medium-sized, yellowish eyes, and the conspicuous pits on the anterior rostrum and upper lips and on the lower lips behind and below the eye. The ventrals are narrower than in most land

R.B. Stuebing

R.B. Stuebing

(Above). *Python reticulatus* and (below). Close-up of head.

snakes. There are 70–80 smooth rows of scales. Ventrals from 309–323 (males) and 309–321 (females); paired subcaudals 88–96 (males) and 85–95 (females). Upper labials 12–15. Both sexes possess a small pair of claws, slightly larger in males, flanking the vent. The top of the head is brown with a dark streak down the middle. The sides of the head are lighter in colour, and there is a dark stripe running diagonally from behind the eye to the side of the neck. The chin is white with a few scattered dark flecks. The body is tan to brown, with a dark, chain-shaped pattern running down the back, edged in golden-yellow. Along the sides below each link are a row of diamond-shaped dark spots with white centres. The ventrals are cream just below the neck, but have increasing amounts of dark mottling towards the rear part of the body.

Reticulate pythons are among most common snakes in Borneo, occurring in almost all lowland habitats, including towns. Though generally terrestrial, they are also common near rivers. Pythons up to four metres in length are not unusual. They feed on a wide variety of warm-blooded vertebrates, and large pythons can be pests of livestock such as chickens and pigs. A large female can lay up to 100 eggs, and stays with them until hatching. The muscle mass of the jaws forms a prominent bulge behind the eyes and ensures a powerful grip with a set of fearsomely long, recurved teeth.

Xenopeltidae

Xenopeltis unicolor
Iridescent Earth Snake; Sunbeam Snake

The type came from Java, but this species is now known from Java to Burma and the Philippines, and all areas in between. It has been found throughout the lowlands of Borneo. *Xeno* = strange, and *peltis* = skin or hide. The reference is to the strange iridescence of the skin, which also accounts for the common name. *Uni* = one, and *color* = hue; referring to the unpatterned adults.

A shiny, smooth, medium-sized, relatively thick-bodied snake with the head almost the same diameter as the neck. Maximum length is a bit over one

R.F. Inger

R.F. Inger

(Above). *Xenopeltis unicolor* and (below). Close-up of head.

metre. The tail is very short—only about 10% of the total—and ends in a pointed tip. The eye is very small. The scales of the head have several unusual features: the preocular (the scale immediately in front of the eye) is very large, larger than the supraocular (the scale above the eye), and curling onto the top surface of the head; there is no loreal (the scale that usually separates the preocular from the nasal scale); and the parietal scales at the rear of the upper surface of the head do not meet. The body scales are smooth and in 15 rows the full length before the tail. Ventrals 177–185 (males), 175–183 (females); caudals 28–31 (males), 27–32 (females); upper labials eight, with the fourth and fifth touching the eye. Adults are uniform brown or blackish above. The entire underside, including the lowest one or two scale rows, is white sometimes with small brown spots. The third and fourth scales rows are usually edged with white. Juveniles have a wide white collar around the rear of the head and neck; gradually brown colour invades the light area so that it disappears by the time the snake reaches 50–60 cm.

Xenopeltis is a secretive snake of swampy coastal areas, including flooded rice fields, and lowland rain forests up to about 700 metres above sea level. It is completely terrestrial and often burrows in mud. The diet consists mainly of frogs, lizards, and snakes, although Tweedie said that it will feed on mice in captivity. This non-aggressive snake is often killed by traffic as it crosses roads between flooded fields.

Xenophidiidae
Spine-Jawed Snake

This family was established in November, 1998, based on two specimens representing two species of small snakes, one species from Thailand and the one from Borneo described below. It is possible that they have some distant relationship to the boas and pythons, but this is far from certain.

Xenophidion acanthognathus
Bornean Spine-Jawed Snake

The type and only specimen known was collected in forest in southwestern Sabah. *Xeno* = strange, *ophidion* = snake; the generic name refers to the difficulty herpetologists are having trying to unravel the evolutionary relationships of this small group of species. *Acantho* = spine, *gnathus* = jaw, referring to a large spiny projection running from the upper jaw to the palatal bone; this spine is not visible unless one dissects a preserved specimen.

This is a small species, with a length of 35 cm, one-sixth of which is tail. The head is slightly flattened, the snout broadly rounded, and the eye small. There is one pair of very large scales on the top of the head immediately behind the nasal scales, which meet in the mid-line. All other scales on the top and side of the head are much smaller. There is no enlarged frontal or parietal scales, such as characterize virtually all species of the family Colubridae. The body scales, except for the two lowest rows, are keeled and arranged in 23 rows at mid-body. The anal plate is undivided as are the subcaudals. Ventrals 181; subcaudals 51; upper labials eight, the third and fourth touching the eye. The general colour is brownish with a zigzag longitudinal pattern. The head is medium brown speckled with lighter colour. Behind the head and running for about three head lengths is a wide white band. Behind that band, the mid-line of the back has a zigzag brown stripe, bordered on the side by a zigzag tan stripe and a darker zigzag stripe. The belly is black with small squarish yellow spots.

The only specimen was found under moss covering a rock in selectively logged forest at 600 m above sea level. It is a female containing enlarged eggs. Food habits are unknown, but the small eye and the many tiny sensory organs on the scales of the snout suggest that it hunts in the forest floor litter. It has a large, stout tooth at the front of the lower jaw which makes it likely that the prey consists of small vertebrates capable of strong struggles.

Acrochordidae

The Acrochordidae is a family consisting of two aquatic snakes of the genus *Acrochordus*, one of which inhabits muddy coastal rivers and peat swamps, while the other is marine. Both have unusual skin, in which there is a pointed bony denticle at the centre of each scale, forming a surface similar to extremely coarse sandpaper or a file. These two species, in fact, are commonly referred to as "file snakes." The skin is loose, almost baggy, and there are no enlarged scales, either ventrals or subcaudals. They possess a blunt snout, relatively small eyes and valvular nostrils, and both eyes and nostrils shifted towards the top of the head. Both species eat fish, and are extremely sluggish, though they are know to bite.

Acrochordus granulatus
Marine File Snake

The type locality is India, but this species is common in coastal areas throughout South-east Asia from Sumatra and Java to the Philippines. It is a common snake around Borneo. *Acro* = outermost, *chorda* = cord, rope; *granulatus* from *granum* = grain.

This is a small snake, rarely reaching a metre in total length, and most specimens seen in Borneo have been considerably less than one metre long. The rather odd-looking head is short, and rounded, and the same diameter as the neck. The eyes are tiny, and the nostrils slightly raised. The entire head is covered with bumpy, granular scales. There are no enlarged ventrals or subcaudals. The head is unmarked and black, while (in Borneo) the upper body is banded black and greyish or whitish in the fashion of the hydrophiine sea snakes. The bands are broadest along the top midline, and taper sharply on the sides. There is a fold of skin along the middle of the belly for most of the body length. The tail is slightly oval in cross-section, and pointed.

R.B. Stuebing

Acrochordus granulatus. Close up of head.

R.B. Stuebing

Acrochordus granulatus

Acrochordus granulatus is regularly seen in trawls for prawns along with hydrophiines such as *Aipysurus eydouxii* and *Lapemis curtus*. It also occurs inshore on tidal flats not far from the beach, where it apparently feeds on bottom-living fish such as gobies. This species is extremely sluggish, hardly moving if disturbed. It rarely if ever bites.

Acrochordus javanicus
Riverine File Snake, Elephant's Trunk Snake

The type locality is Bantam, West Java. This species is widely distributed throughout South-east Asia in coastal areas. In Borneo, most records have been from western Sarawak. "*Javanicus*" = from Java.

This snake attains considerable size, reaching about two metres in total length, with a tail from 18–20% of that length. Its girth is its most impressive feature, and is the reason for the common name. The head is broad behind the eyes, marginally wider than the neck, and with a short, squarish snout. The eyes are small and slightly protruding, and positioned towards the top of the

(Above). *Acrochordus javanicus*. (Below). Close-up of head.

head. The top of the head is covered with the tiny, rough scales similar to but smaller than the ones on the body. There are about 130–150 scale rows, and no enlarged ventrals or subcaudals. The tail is pointed. The head is brown, with a light cross-band just behind the eyes, and a light-edged dark band running from just behind the eye posteriorly across the angle of the jaw. The lips are cream-coloured with some brown blotches; the chin is pale. The upper body is brown; there is a broad dark irregular band along the sides accentuated by a cream-coloured border above and below. The belly is whitish to cream with large round dark blotches.

Acrochordus javanicus is common in the lower reaches of muddy rivers, emerging at night to feed on catfish and eels. Tweedie reports that females can produce 40–50 eggs, portion of develop fully in the oviduct and the young are born "alive".

This snake will apparently bite if mishandled, but usually does not. It is sold in markets in Sarawak for food, and the skin is also used for leather.

Colubridae
Colubrid Snakes [19]

Xenodermatinae

Stoliczkaia borneensis
Stoliczka's Water Snake

The first specimen of this species was said to come from "Kina Balu." Although it has not been reported since 1899 when it was discovered, we found one on MountTrus Madi, Sabah, several years ago. The generic name honours Ferdinand Stoliczka, a well-known 19th century collector of amphibians and reptiles in Central, South and South-east Asia. The species name refers to the origin of the first specimen.

This is a medium-sized snake, very slender, with its body flattened from side to side and with sharply ridged back. Total length reaches one metre, of which the tail forms 30%. The head is much wider than the neck and the snout is broadly rounded and flattened above. The nostril is large and flaring, but the eye is small. The scalation is very peculiar. *Stoliczkaia borneensis* has large scales or shields on the head of the sort found in all advanced, harmless snakes. But in this species there are two rows of small scales crossing the top of the head just in front of the eyes separating the prefrontals (large snout shields) from the frontal (usually the largest shield on the head, situated between the eyes). It is the only Bornean snake with this scale pattern. The temporal scales (on the side of the head near the rear), which in most snakes are larger than the body scales, are quite small. The caudals, the scales under

---

[19] This rather old family includes such a broad diversity of sizes, shapes and ecological roles that categorising them with a single descriptive name is difficult.

77

R.B. Stuebing

R.B. Stuebing

(Above). *Stoliczkaia borneensis* and (below). Close-up of head.

the tail, are single, rather than paired as in the great majority of snakes. The body scales are strongly keeled with tiny knobs on the keels. There are 33–35 rows of scales at mid-body, reducing to 25 before the tail. Ventral scales 205–210 (females only); caudals 117–124; upper labials 11, with the sixth and seventh touching the eye. The head and body are dark brown with black squares forming a checker board pattern. There are several dark vertical bars on the rear of the head. The underside is medium brown, and unmarked.

The snake we found was in the Pangas River on Mount Trus Madi at approximately 800 metres above sea level. As the original specimen (the type) and one other came from "Kina Balu," it appears that this is a montane species. Nothing is known about the diet. The small eye and large nostril suggest that this species hunts by smell, probably at night. The skin of the neck is very loose between the scales and probably allows this species to ingest relatively large prey. Apparently, some individuals have bright blue markings, while others are almost entirely dark brown to black.

Xenelaphis ellipsifer
Ornate Brown Snake

This species was based on a specimen collected in the headwaters of the Sarawak River, and Sarawak remains the only certain area of distribution in Borneo. There is a report of one specimen from "Kinabalu," but that report needs confirmation. The species has been found a few times in Peninsular Malaysia and once in Sumatra. *Ellips* = ellipse, *fer* = bearing, referring to the elliptic markings on the back.

This is a large snake, The few that have been caught were all two metres or a bit longer. The tail is long, about 30% of the total length. The snout is broadly rounded. The eye is large, about twice the length of the distance between the eye and the mouth. Subocular scales separate the eye from the upper labials in some individuals. The scales are smooth and in 17 rows at mid-body. Ventral scales 186–203 (males); subcaudals 129–134 (males); upper labials 8–9, the fourth touching the eye or separated by subocular scales. The species is medium brown above, and the head is unmarked, though the neck may have dark longitudinal streaks. The body has 18–20 large dark brown, black-edged elliptic or almost circular markings. These are separated by narrow, lighter, almost cream-coloured spaces. There are smaller, irregular black spots low on the sides. The belly is white, usually with dark spots at the outer edges of some ventral scales.

79

Very little is known of this forest species. Of the few records that we have, all are from hilly country up to about 1000 metres above sea level. The diet is unknown, but it probably consists of small mammals.

Xenelaphis hexagonotus
Malaysian Brown Snake

This species was originally described from Penang, Peninsular Malaysia. It is abundant in Peninsular Malaysia and also occurs in the southern part of Indochina, Sumatra, and Java. In Borneo it has been found in Kalimantan and

Xenelaphis hexagonotus.

R.B. Stuebing

Sarawak, and probably occurs throughout the island. *Xeno* = strange or foreign, *elaphis* = a kind of snake; *hexagonotus* = six-sided, referring to the shape of the slightly enlarged vertebral scales.

This is a large snake reaching a length of two metres, though most adults are about 1.5 m. The tail is relatively long, about 35–37% of the total length. The snout is rounded. The eye is moderate, its diameter larger than the distance to the mouth, but smaller than the length of the snout. In some individuals, the eye is separated from the upper labials by a row of small subocular scales. The body scales are smooth and arranged in 17 rows at mid-body. The scales of the vertebral row are slightly larger than the adjacent ones and have a hexagonal shape. Ventral scales 185–190 (males), 187–195 (females); subcaudals 157–169 (males), 162–169 (females); upper labials 7–8, the fourth touching the eye or separated from the eye by subocular scales. The head and body are dark green to olive-brown, slightly lighter towards the rear. The belly is yellowish to deep yellow. Beginning at the rear of the head and continuing part way down the body are narrow black vertical bars or triangles whose lower ends encroach on the sides of the belly. In lighter individuals the black markings appear the full length of the snake and extend across the back.

The Brown Snake (actually rather greenish in Borneo) is a ground-dwelling snake of lowland forests. Most of the Sarawak snakes we have seen have come from flattish, wet forests or disturbed areas, while a Sabah specimen was from a coastal area of disturbed peat swamp. This species is an important predator on rats, and in Peninsular Malaysia seems to be one of the most effective rat killers among snakes there. However, a specimen collected near Membakut on the west coast of Sabah had a freshly eaten walking catfish, *Clarias teijsmanni*, in its stomach. In Sarawak, it is called "*beluai*", and considered rather tasty as soup.

Xenodermus javanicus
Rough-Backed Litter Snake

The original specimen came from Java, but this species occurs in Peninsular Malaysia and Sumatra, as well. In Borneo, it has been found in Sabah and Sarawak. We suspect that it is widespread in Borneo. *Xeno* = strange, *derma* = skin; reference is to the strange scalation. The specific name refers to the origin of the first specimen.

(Above). *Xenodermus javanicus* and (below). Close-up of head.

Xenodermus javanicus is a small, slender species, rarely exceeding 60 cm in total length. The scales of the body are very small except for three rows of moderately large, keeled scales down the centre of the back and another row of enlarged, keeled scales on each side separated from the other three by four or five very small scales. The ventral scales are typical of those of most snakes, but the subcaudal scales and the anal plate are single. The head scales are equally distinctive. The only enlarged scales on top of the head are the internasals and prefrontals (Fig. 4D); all the other head scales, including the labial scales, are very small. No other Bornean snake matches that description. The eye is small, its diameter being less than half its distance from the nostril. The nasal scale is very large surrounding the flaring nostril, which points obliquely forward. Ventral scales 162–170; subcaudals 127–134; upper labials 16–17, none touching the eye. The head and body are dark brown or dark grey, without markings. The underside is pale brown or grey, each ventral with a dark band across its front edge.

All Bornean and peninsular records are from lowland rain forest. We have seen this species only at night on or under dead leaves on the forest floor, within 10 metres of the edge of small streams. In Java *Xenodermus javanicus* has been found from 500 to 1000 metres above sea level, most often at the edge of harvested rice fields where it was feeding on frogs. It lays from two to four eggs.

Pareatinae

Aplopeltura boa
Blunt-Headed Tree Snake

This species was described originally from West Java, but is found from southern Thailand through Sumatra, Java, and into the southern Philippines. It is widespread in Borneo. The generic name is from *aploos* = single, *pelta* = shield, and *oura* = tail; the reference is to the single subcaudals under the tail. The species name is the Latin word for a large snake, which in this case is not entirely suitable.

A small, slender snake with body conspicuously flattened from side to side. The head is blunt and much wider than the body. Maximum length is about 80 cm, with the tail comprising one-third or more of the total. The eye is very large, its diameter being greater than the length of the snout. There is no central groove under the chin. A row of small scales separates the eye from the upper labials. There are 13 smooth rows of scales, with the vertebral row (the central one) much larger than the others. The subcaudals are not paired, but single. Ventrals 161–171 (males), 163–173 (females); subcaudals 114–131 (males), 112–127 (females); anal single; upper labials 8–10. The general colour is light chocolate to dark greyish brown, usually with dark-edged saddles on the back. The side may have a row of large white spots. The top of the head is dark brown, but the lip is usually white or cream coloured with a dark triangular area below the eye. Some individuals are quite dark, lacking white areas on the lip and side. The underside is brownish to dark grey.

This forest snake is confined to the lowlands, below 1000 m. It is a nocturnal shrub and bush-dweller and feeds on snails, and sometimes small lizards. The hooklike lower jaw seems to have been modified for eating the former. It has a remarkable ability to extend much of its body horizontally as it moves from branch to branch. If it is threatened, the front third or so of the body becomes rigid so that, with its mottled pattern, it resembles a slender twig. *Aplopeltura boa* apparently lays four or five eggs.

C.L. Chan

(Above and opposite). *Aplopeltura boa.*

84

C.L. Chan

Pareas
Slug-Eating Snake

The species of this genus are small, rarely exceeding half a metre, and brown with various patterns. So far as is known, all feed on snails and slugs. All hide under dead leaves and other debris on the forest floor by day and emerge at night to hunt their prey. Several species climb into low shrubs and herbs to forage. All these species, and their relative *Aplopeltura,* share one peculiarity. The vast majority of snakes have scales under the chin in pairs with a groove down the centre separating the right and left scales. There is no such groove in *Pareas* and *Aplopeltura*; instead rather large scales form an overlapping pattern on the chin and throat. Another unusual feature of these snakes is the undivided anal scale. *Pareas* is the name of a kind of snake in ancient Greece.

Pareas laevis
Blunt-Headed Tree Snake, Smooth Slug-Eating Snake

Described originally from Java, this species has also been recorded from Sumatra and Peninsular Malaysia. In Borneo it is widely distributed in all forested areas. *Laevis* = smooth, referring to the smooth scales.

A small snake slightly flattened from side to side, with small, blunt head and a short tail. Maximum size about 40 cm. The midline of the back is keeled and the scales in this position (the vertebral row) are a bit larger than adjacent scales. The scales are smooth even under magnification and are in 15 rows the length of the body. The eyes protrude from the side of the head and seem to be pointed forwards. The diameter of the eye is shorter than the snout, but longer than the distance between the eye and the lip. There is no preocular scale before the eye; instead the eye and nasal scale (the scale perforated by the nostril) are separated by a single low scale, the loreal. Ventrals 152–161 (males), 158–165 (females); subcaudals 41–47 (males), 36–40 (females); upper labials 5, third and fourth bordering eye. The general colour is medium to dark brown, with many narrow, vertical darker bars on the body. The vertical bars do not cross over the midline of the back, but do extend onto the belly forming dark spots on the edges of some of the ventral scales. The head is usually slightly darker than the body, but lacks lines or bars. The underside of the head is usually the same brown as the side of the body. The belly is white or straw-coloured except for the dark spots that form the ends of the dark bars on the sides.

This common species occurs in forests from near sea level to as high as 1150 metres above sea level. At night it crawls over the forest floor searching out slugs that form the main part of its diet. During the day it retreats under dead leaves.

Pareas vertebralis, a rather common species in the Cameron Highlands of Peninsular Malaysia, is very similar to *Pareas laevis* in shape, head scalation, and coloration. The main differences involve numbers of ventral and caudal scales; *P. vertebralis* has higher scale counts. The only Bornean locality recorded for *Pareas vertebralis* is Mount Kinabalu; we suspect the two specimens reported are actually *Pareas laevis*.

R.B. Stuebing

Pareas laevis.

Pareas malaccanus
Dark-Necked Slug-Eating Snake

Originally described from "Malacca", which 150 years ago might have meant simply the Malay Peninsula. The species is also known from Sumatra and islands off its west coast. In Borneo, it has been reported from Sabah, Sarawak, and one locality in south-eastern Kalimantan. It probably occurs throughout the island. *Malaccanus* = from Malacca.

A small, heavy-bodied snake, with a rather prominent keel down the centre of the back. Maximum size is around 60 cm. The head is slightly wider than the neck, and the snout is blunt. The eye is small, its diameter is shorter

Pareas malaccanus.

88

than the snout and shorter than the distance separating the eye from the lip. The eye and nasal scale are separated by one scale, the loreal. The body scales appear to be smooth, but with a microscope a faint keel can be seen on each scale. The scale row on the centre of the back (the vertebral row) is very slightly larger than adjacent rows. Ventrals 165–181 (males), 179 (female); subcaudals 42–58 (males), 35 (female); upper labials 7, third and fourth border the eye. The general colour is light brown with many vertical, dark bars, 2–4 scales wide on the body. The bars do not continue across the vertebral scale row. The head is a bit darker than the body, has dark edging on some scales, but lacks any distinct lines. The most conspicuous pattern element is a dark brown or black band on the neck and fore part of the body. The band, which is several times the head length, almost encircles the body having a narrow gap along the vertebral scale row and a narrow line down the centre of the underside. The dark area extends forward to cover at least the sides of the throat. The belly behind the dark band is straw-coloured or tan, speckled with small, irregular dark brown spots. *P. malaccanus* differs from others in the genus by the dark band encircling the front of the body and the distinctly keeled back.

This species is characteristic of lowland forests, but ranges as high as 1000 metres above sea level. At night it climbs on low shrubs and herbaceous plants. By day it retreats under dead leaves on the forest floor. The main prey in the diet are slugs.

Pareas nuchalis
Barred Slug-Eating Snake

The type locality is Matang, Sarawak. The species occurs only in Borneo and has been found throughout Sarawak and Kalimantan, and one locality in Sabah. *Nuchalis* = referring to the black mark on the nape.

A small, slender snake with a body flattened from side to side, a long tail about 25% of total length, and a rather short, blunt head. Maximum size is about half a metre. The diameter of the eye is longer than the snout and longer than the distance between the eye and the lip. The eye is separated from the labial scales by a ring of small scales, and is separated from the nasal by two scales, a preocular and the loreal. Like all members of this genus, this species has no groove under the chin and throat. Scales are in 15 rows and appear to be smooth, though under high magnification one can see very faint keels. Scales in the vertebral row are a bit larger than those in adjacent rows. Ventrals 215 (female), 207–218 (males); subcaudals 105–108; upper labials 8–9. General colour tan to medium brown with many, narrow (one or two scales wide), vertical bars on body. The bars do not cross over the centre of the back. The head has a short, slender, oblique black line from the lower rear corner of the eye to the front edge of the last upper labial and usually a thin, vertical black line down the rear of the head. A thin black line runs from the upper rear corner of the eye to the nape of the neck where it joins a large, squarish black spot that covers the nape and that usually has a shallow notch at its rear border. The underside of the head and the belly are light tan or yellowish; the belly usually has very small, irregular dark dots. The coloration of head and neck and the long tail distinguish this species from others in the genus.

This species is part of the lowland rain forest community and has not been found higher than 500 m above sea level. It is active at night and lives in low vegetation, climbing on herbs and low shrubs below two metres above the ground. There is no direct information on diet, but the shape of the head suggests that this species, like its relatives, feeds on snails and slugs.

Pareas carinatus, distributed from Java to Burma and Vietnam, is very similar to *Pareas nuchalis* in coloration and general form. However, *P. carinatus* has fewer ventrals (less than 190) and subcaudals (less than 90). It is possible that all Bornean records of *P. carinatus* refer to specimens of *P. nuchalis*.

Homalopsinae

The Homalopsinae is a subfamily of small to medium-sized semiaquatic snakes which in Borneo includes the genera *Cerberus*, *Enhydris*, *Fordonia* and *Homalopsis*. All have relatively small eyes, and nostrils shifted towards the top of the head. These nostrils are also valvular, e.g., can be opened and closed similar to the adaptation seen in crododilians. The head is completely covered by large shields in all except *Ceberus*. Homalopsines are mostly wetland snakes, inhabiting either freshwater swamps (or even buffalo wallows), and tidal flats of mangrove or *Nipah* palm areas. Although all are rear-fanged and apparently possess a mild venom, there are no reports of serious effects on humans.

Cerberus rynchops
Dog-Faced Water Snake

The type locality is listed as ?Ganjam?, India, but this species is common along coastal areas throughout South-east Asia. *Cerberus* refers to the dog-like monster that guarded the gates of Hades in Roman mythology; *rhynchus* for snout, and *ops* = face or appearance.

Dog-Faced Water Snakes are small snakes rarely reaching a metre in total length, of which about 17–20% is tail. The head is long, considerably wider than the neck, while the snout is short and tapered in front of the eyes. The eye is small, its diameter about one-third its distance to the nostril, and

Cerberus rynchops.

R.B. Stuebing

Cerberus rynchops. Close-up of head.

the pupil round. There are 23 or 25 (sometimes 29) mid-body rows of keeled scales. Ventrals are 153–159 (males), 149–154 (females); subcaudals 52–60 (males), 50–61 (females), anal divided; upper labials, 9–10, the fifth and sixth below the eye but separated from it by a row of small scales. The head is dark brown with a dark stripe on the midline behind the eyes and a dark stripe behind each eye. The upper body is dark brown or olive with indistinct dark crossbars, while the first 2–3 dorsal scale rows are light-coloured, forming a light stripe the length of the body.

The upper lip is dark near the end of the snout, becoming lighter near the angle of the jaw. The chin is dirty white, while the ventral scales are heavily marked with dark brown to black to the tip of the tail.

Cerberus rynchops is extremely common on the mud flats of tidal river estuaries, where it feeds on small fish, such as mudskippers and gobies.

92

Enhydris plumbea
Orange-Bellied Mud Snake

The type locality is Java, and this species is widely distributed throughout South-east Asia. It occurs in Borneo at elevations below 500 metres. *Enhydris* is a Greek word for water-snake; while *plumbea* = lead, perhaps referring to the leaden grey body colour.

Orange-Bellied Mud Snakes are small snakes, usually reaching a total length of less than 50 cm and the tail is from 12–14% of that length. The head is slightly wider than the neck, while the snout is tapered but rather short. The eye is small, its distance to the nostril is about one and a half times its

Enhydris plumbea.

93

diameter, while the pupil is rounded to slightly elliptical. The triangular internasal scale on top of the snout is characteristic of this species. There are 19 rows of smooth scales at mid-body. Ventrals are 122–128 (males), 119–127 (females); subcaudals 33–40 (males), 30–39 (females), anal divided; upper labials 8, the fourth, or fourth and fifth touching the eye. The head and upper body are light grey to greyish brown, and the lips and chin whitish. Many of the dorsal scales are dark-edged, especially on the sides. The belly is unmarked, and ranges from pinkish to light orange.

Enhydris plumbea is common in swampy areas of disturbed vegetation such as drainage ditches, old wet rice fields or even buffalo wallows, where it lives on a diet of frogs and tadpoles. The bite of this species is mildly venomous, and known to cause some numbness, pain and swelling.

Enhydris enhydris is similar in size, but darker above with the chin and throat yellow, with dusky markings. There are a series of dark stripes low on the body, including one down the middle of the belly. All Bornean records of *E. enhydris* are from extreme western Sarawak and West Kalimantan, and there are apparently no recent collections.

Enhydris doriae
Blotch-Lipped Mud Snake

The type locality is Sarawak in western Borneo, and this species is apparently endemic to Borneo, where so far it has been found exclusively in swampy habitats below 500 metres in coastal Sarawak and Sabah. *Doriae* is derived from the name of a 19th Century Genoese nobleman, the Marquis Doria, who supported many herpetological collecting expeditions to Southeast Asia.

Blotch-Lipped Mud Snakes are small to medium-sized snakes reaching a total length of about two-thirds of a metre, of which about 17–20% is tail. The head is slightly wider than the neck, while the snout is short and blunt. The eye is small, its distance to the nostril is about twice its diameter, while the pupil is rounded to slightly oval. The row of small scales under the eye, and some divided upper labial scales are characteristic of this species. There are 31–33 mid-body rows of smooth scales. Ventrals 142–145 (males), 140–155 (females); subcaudals 40–60 (males), 35–49 (females), anal divided; upper labials, 13–16. The head and upper body are grey to greyish brown, and the lips blotched with grey and cream. The tip of the chin is brown, whitish-cream behind, sometimes with scattered dark spots. The belly is mottled with dark spots, which increase towards the middle and rear of the body. The first 2–5 scale rows are light with dark mottling, though the degree varies with individuals.

Enhydris doriae is common in swampy areas or in muddy rivers, and has been found at the same locality in Sabah as *E. plumbea.*

Enhydris punctata has divided upper labials, but does not have a row of small scales under the eye. It has yellow bars on the nape and one between the eyes (specimens from Peninsular Malaysia). In Borneo, it is known only from western and southern Kalimantan. A fourth species, *Enhydris alternans*, was reported from Borneo almost a century ago, but the record needs confirmation. This species is dark brown or black with many narrow yellow bars or rows of small spots crossing the back; its underside is black with wide yellow cross bars.

Fordonia leucobalia
Crab-Eating Water Snake

The type locality is the island of Timor in Indonesia, and this species is known from numerous localities throughout South-east Asia. The origin of the word *fordonia* is unclear, although it may be derived from the Latin, *fordus* meaning pregnant or fertile; *leucos* = white, *balios* = white-spotted.

Crab-Eating Water Snakes are small, rarely reaching a total length exceeding half a metre, of which about 11–15% is tail. The head is barely wider than the neck, while the snout is tapered and slightly rounded. The eye is small, its diameter about twice its distance to the nostril. The pupil is round. The lower jaw of this species is short, and the upper labial scales are folded under the upper jaw. There are 25–29 mid-body rows of smooth scales. Ventrals are 142–150 (males), 144–150 (females); subcaudals 30–41 (males), 28–41 (females), anal divided; upper labials 5, the third touching the eye. The head is greyish brown, while the upper body is greyish. The upper lip is light with some grey mottling at the upper edge. The fore part of the chin is covered in grey, light-edged scales. The belly is creamy white, with some light greyish tinge towards the rear of the body. The first 2–5 scale rows are light with grey mottling, though the degree varies with individuals.

Fordonia leucobalia is found in tidal rivers, where it apparently captures crabs by seeking them in their burrows.

95

Homalopsis buccata
Puff-Faced Water Snake

The type locality is India, though this species is known from Peninsular Malaysia, Sumatra and Java. It appears to be rather uncommon in Borneo, except in western Sarawak and Kalimantan. *Homalos* = equal, and *opsis* = appearance, perhaps referring to the symmetrical markings on the head; *buccata* from *bucca* = cheeks.

Puff-Faced Water Snakes are medium-sized snakes reaching a total length of slightly over one metre, of which tail length is about 20%. The head is conspicuously wider than the neck, appearing almost swollen behind the eyes, while the snout is squarish. The eye is small, its diameter about twice its distance from the nostril. The pupil is round. The lower jaw of this species is slightly shorter than the upper; the mouth is upturned at the angle of the jaw. There are 32–48 mid-body rows of keeled scales. Ventrals 154–169 (males), 158–173 (females); subcaudals 64–95 (males), 68–77 (females), anal divided; upper labials, 10–13, fifth and sixth below the eye, usually separated from it by a small row of scales. The head is light brown, with a dark stripe through the eye, which connects across the back of the head as a broad light brown band. The upper body is greyish with thick, X-shaped reddish brown, dark-edged cross bands, which tend to fade in older adults. The upper and lower lips are grey with light edges. The chin is dirty white, while the belly is dirty white or cream with paired dark spots at the edges of the ventral scales.

Homalopsis buccata is found in rivers, swamps and ponds where it feeds on fish. According to Tweedie, it is often a pest of fish ponds in Peninsular Malaysia.

Lycodontinae

Lepturophis borneensis
Slender-Tailed Wolf Snake

Originally described from Kuching, Sarawak, this species has since been found at many places in Sarawak and Sabah. It probably occurs throughout Borneo. It is also known from Peninsular Malaysia. *Leptos* = thin, *ouros* or

R.F. Inger

Lepturophis borneensis.

uros = tail, and *ophis* = snake; referring to the very slender tail of this snake. The species name, of course, refers to the land where it was found.

This is a medium-sized to long snake, reaching a total length of two metres, but it is slender and so does not appear to be large. The tail is long, accounting for 35–38% of the total length. The head is wider than the neck and has a flat, almost blunt snout. The eye is moderate in size, with its diameter a bit less than the distance between eye and nostril. The body scales are sharply keeled and each keel is set with small knobs giving the keels a saw-like surface. There are 17 scale rows for most of the length, dropping to 15 before the tail. The ventral and subcaudal scales have a strong keel running along near their outer edges. Ventral scales 245–246 (males), 228–232 (females); subcaudals 190–206 (males), 171–176 (females); anal divided; upper labials 8, sometimes 7, with the third to fifth or fourth and fifth bordering the eye. Adults are dark brown above without any markings. The underside of the head, body, and tail are white. Juveniles have a series of 30–40 white rings one or two scales wide around the body and a wider ring at the rear of the head.

97

Lepturophis borneensis is a snake of primary and slightly disturbed forest in both flat and hilly terrain below 500 metres above sea level. The keeled ventrals and subcaudals are typical of many arboreal snakes in Borneo and South-east Asia, but all but one (of the many *Lepturophis*) we have seen were on the ground, on stream banks and gravel beds, or actually swimming. The diet consists mainly of lizards, especially of the semi-aquatic skinks of the genus *Tropidophorus*.

Some workers believe this species is merely the adult of *Lycodon albofuscus*.

Lycodon
Wolf Snakes

The generic name, which means "wolf tooth," comes from the long tooth at the front of the upper jaw of all species of *Lycodon*. This tooth, although it is fang-like, is not grooved, for these are not venomous snakes. Nevertheless, the head is slightly triangular in some species, almost python-like because of the enlarged masseter or jaw muscles. All the members of this genus apparently feed on lizards, and the long tooth probably is important in holding on to active, squirming prey. Other features these species have in common are a vertically elongated pupil and "keeled" or sharply angular ventral scales. All the species are active at night.

Lycodon albofuscus
Dusky Wolf Snake

This species was originally described from Sumatra. In Borneo it is known from a few places in Sabah and Sarawak. *Albo* = white, *fuscus* = dark; referring to the white and black pattern of juveniles.

A slender, medium-sized snake with a flattened head, rounded snout, and bulging eyes. Maximum size is just over one metre, with the tail accounting for about 30% of the total. A preocular scale is present. The scales are keeled and in 17 rows. Ventral scales 238–256; subcaudals 115–208; upper labials 7 or 8, the fourth and fifth touch the eye. The general colour is dark brown or black. Juvenile snakes have a pattern of 35–40 whitish or yellow rings one or two scales wide circling the body and a wider light ring at the rear of the head. The underside is whitish or yellow, without any dark markings. (Some authors have suggested that this species is actually the juvenile of *Leopturophis borneensis*).

Nothing is known of the general biology of this species. The angular ventral scales suggest that it spends part of its life climbing in vegetation above the ground.

Lycodon aulicus
Common Wolf Snake

The origin of the first specimen described is unknown, but this species is certainly widely distributed in southern Asia, from India and southern China to Timor, Sulawesi, and the Philippines. Oddly, it had never been reported

Francis Lim

Lycodon aulicus.

99

from Borneo until a dead one was discovered in the Stuebings' back yard. *Lycodon aulicus* is common around houses over most of its range and its association with man has probably enabled it to "stowaway" in cargo being shipped or carried about.

It is a medium-sized snake, with a flattened head and rounded snout. Maximum length is less than one metre, with the tail being one-fifth of the total. There is a large preocular scale. The scales are smooth and in 17 rows, reducing to 15 near the end of the body. Ventral scales 180–197 (males), 185–209 (females); subcaudals 65–71 (males), 57–70 (females); upper labials 9, the third to fifth or the fourth and fifth touch the eye. Adults are brown or purple brown above. There is usually a narrow yellow band at the rear of the head that is sometimes interrupted or spotted with brown. Some of the scales have light edges that form irregular cross bands. The belly is yellow or whitish.

In Peninsular Malaysia in small towns this species enters houses searching for its main prey, house geckos. Females lay four to seven eggs and are reported to remain close to the clutch.

Lycodon effraenis
Brown Wolf Snake

This species was described originally from Penang in Peninsular Malaysia, and is now known from Sumatra and Borneo, where it seems to be widely distributed. *Effraenis* = unrestrained, presumably referring to the aggressive manner of the first specimen seen by a biologist. An exaggeration.

This is a medium-sized snake, with a flattened head and a broadly rounded, flaring snout. The bulge at the side of the snout is caused by the decidedly enlarged front tooth. Maximum size is about one metre, with the tail about 20% of the total length. The scales are smooth and in 17 rows. The ventrals have a distinct keel near the outer ends. Ventrals 215–220 (males), 225–233 (females); subcaudals 80–102 (males), 87–96 (females); upper labials 9–10, with the third to fifth or fourth to sixth touching the eye. A large preocular scale forms the front border of the eye.

The general colour is a rich chocolate or reddish brown. Younger snakes have yellow rings three to five scales wide encircling the body. As the snakes age, the yellow areas are invaded by brown and larger individuals tend to be completely brown.

R.F. Inger

Lycodon effraenis.

Lycodon effraenis lives in lowland forests below 700 m above sea level. It is an arboreal species, though sometimes seen on the ground.

Lycodon subcinctus
Belted Wolf Snake

Although originally described from Java, the species occurs throughout Malaysia, in most of western Indonesia and the southern Philippines. It has been reported from all parts of Borneo. *Sub* = somewhat, *cinctus* = belted, referring to the wide rings around the body in smaller individuals.

A medium-sized snake, with a broadly rounded snout and flattened head. Maximum size about one metre. The tail is 15–19% of total length. There is no preocular scale, but the loreal scale borders the eye. The scales are very weakly keeled and arranged in 17 rows. Ventral scales 204–220 (males),

202–226 (females; subcaudals 68–80 (males), 57–71 (females); upper labials 8, third to fifth or 4 and fifth border the eye. Black or dark brown. Young snakes have white bands three to five scales wide encircling the body, the first one usually covering the rear half of the head and the neck. As the snakes age, dark pigment invades the white bands so that adults are almost entirely black on the upper surfaces. Often in adults the light bands can be faintly discerned and in most adults vestiges of the white areas persist on the belly.

This forest species occurs from near sea level to about 1000 m. At night it can be seen moving over the floor litter or in vegetation. Like many arboreal species it can climb up the trunks of large trees. *Lycodon subcinctus* lays from five to 11 eggs.

Daryl Karns

Lycodon subcinctus.

Oligodon

These ground dwelling snakes are small to medium-sized, rather slender to almost stocky, with short to moderate tails. All have short heads not distinct from the neck, an upcurved rostral scale at the tip of the snout, and a dark pattern on the head resembling an inverted V or Y. All but one of the Bornean species have undivided anal plates, a relatively uncommon condition in colubrid snakes. One of the unusual features of species of *Oligodon* is a much enlarged rear tooth. That tooth is not grooved and these snakes are not venomous. However, when grasped by a person, they have the ability to rotate the upper jaw and are able to inflict a painful stab with the elongated tooth, often despite being gripped at the neck very firmly. When not molested, these small snakes are inoffensive. The usual function of the large tooth is to grip the hard-scaled skinks that are their usual prey. The large, curved tooth reminded someone of the shape of a Gurkha knife, with the result that these snakes are called "Kukri Snakes". Eight species have been reported from Borneo. One of those species, *Oligodon cinereus*, is included in the Bornean fauna based on a single specimen; since this species is otherwise well known only from the continent north of Peninsular Malaysia, we suspect that the Bornean record is a case of misidentification. Another species, *Oligodon annulifer* (see below), may be merely the young of another species. *Oligo* = few, *don* = tooth, referring to the low number of teeth in the upper jaw.

Key to species of *Oligodon* from Borneo

1   Body with stripes 2
    Body without stripes 3

2   Dark stripes without light spots .... *Oligodon octolineatus*
    Small red or yellow or white spots in dark vertebral stripe ....
    .... *Oligodon everetti*
    .... *Oligodon vertebralis*

3   Ventrals barred with dark pattern .... *Oligodon purpurascens*
    Ventrals unmarked or if spotted, only at outer edges 4

4   Body with about 25 black rings, each with an oval yellowish spot ....
.... *Oligodon annulifer*
Body without black rings or crossbars 5

5   Narrow brownish or reddish crossbars on back; 15 scale rows ....
.... *Oligodon signatus*
Narrow whitish crossbars on back; 17 scales rows ....
.... *Oligodon subcarinatus*

Oligodon annulifer
Spotted Kukri Snake

The type specimen came from "North Borneo," where it was collected by A.H. Everett who also collected the type of *Oligodon everetti* (see below). This species has not been reported by anyone since 1893, when it was described. The species name means "bearing rings" from *annulus* = ring, and *fer* = bear or carry.

The type and only known specimen was a juvenile only 16 cm long, with the tail less than one-fifth of the total. The smooth scales are in 15 rows. Ventral scales 153; subcaudals 49; upper labials seven, with the third and fourth touching the eye. The anal plate is undivided.

The general colour is brown, with 26 black rings across the back. Each ring encloses a large oval yellowish spot. The sides are black-spotted. The belly is white with a row of small black spots on each side. This colour description was based on the preserved type specimen; the light spots may be reddish in life and the ground colour reddish brown.

We suspect that the type specimen is a juvenile of another species, likely to be *O. everetti*.

Oligodon everetti
Jeweled Kukri Snake

Described from Mount Kinabalu, this species has been found at various places in the lowlands of Sabah. It probably occurs over most of Borneo. It

Biorn Lardner

Oligodon everetti.

has not been observed elsewhere. This species was named after the collector of the first specimen, A.H. Everett.

A small slender species, probably never exceeding 50 cm. The tail tapers gradually to a sharp point and is distinctly longer in males (about one-third of total length) than in females (about one-fifth of total). Ventral scales 132–138 (males), 152–154 (females); subcaudals 67–72 (males), 46–52 (females); upper labials 7, with third and fourth touching the eye. Body with three black stripes on a grey-brown background. The black stripe down the centre of the back is three scales wide and encloses a series of white and coral bars. The lower stripe on each side encloses white spots. The top of the head has a dark brown V-shaped mark pointing forwards, with the arms passing down to the throat. A second dark brown mark crosses the snout, passing through the eyes. The entire underside is coral red.

Oligodon everetti lives on the floor of lowland forests, though the first specimen, from "Mount Kina Balu", may have come from above 1000 metres. The bright red belly seems to mimic some venomous leaf litter snakes, such as coral snakes (*Maticora*). One *O. everetti* was found with a floor-dwelling skink (*Sphenomorphus*) in its stomach.

105

Oligodon vertebralis is very similar to *O. everetti* in coloration and in scalation. The only differences involve a slightly shorter tail in males of *vertebralis* and the scale at the vent. In *vertebralis* the anal scale is divided; in *everetti* it is undivided. More specimens from Kalimantan may show these to be a single species. *Oligodon annulifer* (p. 104) is known from a single juvenile snake from "North Borneo, and resembles *O. everetti* in scalation, but has dark rings on the body enclosing large, oval, yellowish brown spots.

Oligodon octolineatus
Striped Kukri Snake

The exact type locality is uncertain, but this species is well known from Peninsular Malaysia, Sumatra, Java, and all states in Borneo. *Octo* = eight, *lineatus* = lines or stripes, referring to the pattern.

A small, slender snake, with a moderately short tail. Maximum known length is about 60cm, with the tail accounting for between one-sixth and one-fifth of the total. The scales are smooth and in 17 rows the length of the body. Ventral scales 160–172 (males), 174–185 (females); subcaudals 46–60

Oligodon octolineatus.

R.B. Stuebing

106

(males), 42–52 (females); upper labials 6, with the third and fourth touching the eye. Pale brownish, with three pairs of dark brown stripes, the upper-most pair the widest and enclosing a narrow red or reddish brown stripe down the centre of the back. The uppermost dark stripes join on top of the head and project forward onto the snout as an arrow-shaped mark, with arms passing through the eyes. An oblique dark brown stripe runs from the top of the head behind the eye to the throat. The unmarked underside is usually pink.

This is a very abundant little snake in some areas. Although primarily a forest species, it wanders into gardens and occasionally into houses. Most common at elevations near sea level, it has been found as high as 1000 metres. Although small and seemingly inoffensive, it usually bites when handled, and has an uncanny ability to twist the head into any position to do so.

Oligodon purpurascens
Maroon Kukri Snake

Originally described from Java, this species is now also known from Peninsular Malaysia, Sumatra, and Borneo. It has been reported from Sabah, Sarawak, and Kalimantan. *Purpur* = purple, *ascens* = tinged, referring to the general colour.

A medium-sized, rather stocky species. The maximum known size is just under one metre. The tail is relatively short, accounting for about one-seventh of the total length. The smooth scales are in 19 rows until just before the end of the body where the number is reduced to 15. Ventral scales 164–179 (males), 173–177 (females); subcaudals 46–51 (males), 43–48 (females); upper labials 8, the fourth and fifth touching the eye. The general colour is purplish brown, with a series of large, black-edged, dark brown blotches down the back. Between blotches there are two or three narrow, black, zigzag, vertical lines. In some individuals the pattern is reduced to the vertical zigzag lines. The underside is yellow or pink (bright coral red in juvenile snakes), with black pigment covering half the width or the entire width of alternate ventrals.

Oligodon purpurascens is mainly a hill species found in primary and secondary forests. In Borneo it is most abundant between 200 and 600 metres above sea level, but one was seen at 1100 metres on the Kota Kinabalu-Tambunan Road in Sabah.

107

R.B. Stuebing

Bjorn Lardner

(Above). *Oligodon purpurascens* and (below). Close-up of head.

Oligodon signatus
Rusty-Banded Kukri Snake

This species was found originally on Singapore Island, but has since been reported from Peninsular Malaysia and Sumatra, and now from Borneo. The only Bornean record we know of is from Sabah. *Signatus* = marked with a pattern.

A small, slender snake reaching a maximum length of less than 60 cm. The tail is relatively short, forming about one-sixth of the total, and tapers to a sharp point. The smooth scales are in 15 rows the full length of the body. Specimens from Peninsular Malaysia have 17 rows. Ventral scales 157 (female); subcaudals 43; upper labials 7, with the third and fourth touching the eye. Most of the body is reddish brown, with a series of long, light tan ovals down the centre of the back and a series of light tan vertical bars low on the side. Looking down on the snake, it appears to have a series of reddish crossbars. On the fore part of the body, the reddish brown areas point forwards and on the neck this colour projects on the head as a slender V with the arms crossing the eyes. There is an oblique dark brown bar from the top of the head behind the eye to the throat. The underside is yellowish, with small dark brown squares at the outer edges of half of the ventral scales.

Almost nothing known of the habits of this species. The only Bornean specimen obtained so far came from primary forest at 350 metres above sea level.

Oligodon subcarinatus
Barred Kukri snake

This species was described from Sarawak more than a hundred years ago and has been seen only a few times since then in Sabah and Sarawak. *Sub* = somewhat, *carinatus* = keeled, referring to the feeble keeling of some scales.

This is a small, slender species with a maximum known length of less than 45 cm. The tail is slender and moderate in length, accounting for one-fifth of the total length in both sexes. The scales are in 17 rows until near the end of the body and appear to be smooth. Under a microscope, one to three scale rows can be seen to have weak keels. Ventral scales 154–158; subcaudals 50–57 (both sexes); uppper labials 7, the third and fourth touching the eye. Back and sides dark brown, with 20–30 light sandy crossbars. These bars are widened near the midline, with orange-red occupying the middle six scale rows. The top of the head has dark brown spots forming a broken V pattern. A dark bar crosses the snout and passes through the eyes. The underside is orange-red with a few scattered, small dark spots.

The only specimens we have seen were found under logs in primary rain forest around 200 metres above sea level.

Psammodynastes
Mock Vipers

Both species of this genus have viper-like heads—enlarged, flat on top, and steep sided. Two or three teeth at the front of the jaw and two or three at the rear are much enlarged and fang-like, though these snakes are not venomous; however, they are quick to bite when disturbed. The front teeth are large enough to cause a distinct bulge in the lip. These snakes are small, never exceeding 60–65 cm, and have short tails about one-fifth of total length. The two species are very similar to one another and are not easily distinguished. *Psammodynastes pictus* has the first lower labials meeting in the midline under the chin, whereas in *P. pulverulentus* the lower labials are separated by the chin shields. The top of the head is striped in *P. pulverulentus* but not in *P. pictus*.

The generic name is derived from *psammos* = sand, and *dynastes* = ruler. These snakes, which do not live in sandy country, were first placed in the genus *Psammophis*, a group living mainly in sandy, arid areas that could account for the unsuitable first part of the present name.

Psammodynastes pictus
Painted Mock Viper

Originally described from Sumatra, *Psammodynastes pictus* has also been found in Peninsular Malaysia, Singapore, and Borneo, where it is widely distributed. *Pictus* = painted, presumably referring to the stripes on the body in some individuals.

John Murphy

Psammodynastes pictus.

A small snake, with an enlarged, viper-like head and with a short tail. Maximum reported length is 65 cm; the tail makes up one-fifth of the total. The eye is large, larger than its distance from the nostril. There is one loreal scale between the nasal and preocular scales. The enlarged front teeth cause a bulge in the lip. The first lower labial scales meet at the midline. The body scales are smooth and in 17 rows at mid-body. Ventral scales 153–178 (males), 155–175 (females); subcaudals 72–80 (males), 66–79 (females); upper labials eight, with the third to fifth touching the eye. The general colour is brown to dark grey, marked in various ways with darker pigment. In most individuals, a dark brown or black stripe runs back from the snout through the eye on to the body, but the stripe ends just behind the neck in most Bornean specimens. The commonest body pattern consists of a wide dark brown or black band down the centre of the back interrupted by light areas of varying widths. There is usually a second, lower dark band on the side, also interrupted with light bars. In some snakes the predominant colour is dark brown or black with narrow light cross bars in three or four staggered rows. The underside is grey or light brown, heavily speckled with small black and white spots. The body stripes are more conspicuous in juveniles.

This nocturnal species lives in lowland rain forest; all known records are from below 600 metres above sea level. It is usually seen on low vegetation

111

along small streams, where it feeds on small fishes and frogs. It can lay from five to seven eggs.

Psammodynastes pulverulentus
Dusky Mock Viper

Originally described from Java, this species is known to occur from southern China and Burma to the Philippines and Lesser Sunda Islands. It is widely distributed in Borneo. *Pulveris* = dusty, and *lentus* = full of, referring to the dusky coloration.

C.L. Chan

Psammodynastes pulverulentus.

Psammodynastes pulverulentus is small snake with a short tail. Maximum length is about 60 cm, with the tail accounting for about one-fifth. The head is enlarged and viper-like, with a flat top and vertical sides to the snout. The eye is large, larger than its distance to the nostril, and has a vertically elliptic pupil. There are two superimposed loreal scales between the nasal and preocular scales. All of the lower labial scales are separated at the mid-line by the chin shields. The smooth body scales are in 17 rows at mid-body. Ventral scales 162–165 (males), 166–189 (females); subcaudals 59–66 (males), 58–61 (females); upper labials eight, with the third to fifth touching the eye. The body is grey to light brown with narrow blackish crossbars separated alternately by brown and grey areas. A dark brown stripe runs from the snout through the eye to the neck. The top of the head has a striped pattern which begins as a dark brown line on the centre of the neck running forward as a branch above each eye, while a second stripe begins between the eyes and runs forward to the tip of the snout. A short dark stripe usually flanks the first one over the temple. The underside is grey or light brown, heavily speckled with darker pigment.

Psammodynastes pulverulentus lives in rain forest below 750 metres above sea level. It is nocturnal and moves through the forest usually on low vegetation and feeds almost exclusively on lizards. It is an irritable small snake and will form defensive coils and strike in viper-like fashion if threatened. Its bite is painful but not dangerous. It has been known to produce from three to ten young.

R.B. Stuebing

Psammodynastes pulverulentus.

113

Colubrinae

Ahaetulla fasciolata
Banded Vine Snake

This snake was found first in the south-eastern corner of Kalimantan, but has been collected in eastern Sabah and various parts of Sarawak. It has also been reported from Sumatra and the Natuna Islands. *Ahaetulla*—of unknown origin and meaning; *fasciolata*, from *fascia* = band.

A medium-sized, slender snake with an elongate, thin tail and drawn out, narrow snout. Maximum size is about 1.5 m, with the tail comprising 34–37% of the total. The long, narrow snout is more than twice the diameter of the eye. is blunt at the tip, and ends in a curled up rostral scale. The eye is large and has a horizontal pupil. There is a pronounced, long groove on the side of the snout from the front margin of the eye to the nostril, which is located near the tip of the snout. The scales are in 15 rows until near the end of the body, where the number is reduced to 13. The scales of the vertebral row are distinctly larger than the others. Ventral scales 206–222 (males), 194–235 (females); subcaudals 178–204 (males), 179–206 (females); upper labials 8 or 9, the fourth to sixth touching the eye. Light brown or pinkish above;, with many narrow, oblique, dark bands crossing the first half or two-thirds of the body. In very large adults the bands may be obscure. The belly is dark grey with a thin light line on each side near the ends of the ventrals. The head is light grey with many curved or elongate dark spots.

The Banded Vine Snake lives in shrubs and trees in primary or secondary rain forests from near sea level to about 1000 metres. Little is known of the habits of this species, but presumably they resemble those of *Ahaetulla prasina* (see below).

Ahaetulla prasina
Green Vine Snake

Originally described from Java, this species has been found throughout South-east Asia and in the East Indies as far as Sulawesi and the Lesser Sundas. It occurs throughout Borneo. *Prasinus* = the green colour of a leek.

114

R.B. Stuebing

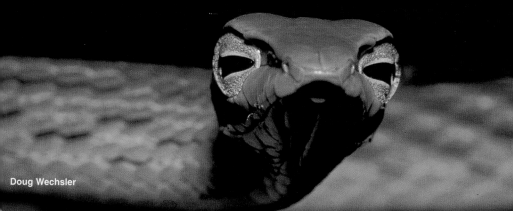

Doug Wechsler

(Above). *Ahaetulla prasina* and (below). Close-up of head.

C.L. Chan

A long, slender snake, with a thin, drawn-out tail and a long, narrow snout. Maximum size is about 2 m, with the tail accounting for 37–39% of the total. Like the preceding species, the snout is twice the diameter of the eye and ends with the rostral curved upward with a free edge. The eye has a horizontal pupil and is preceded by a groove on the side of the snout. The smooth scales are in 15 rows, reducing to 13 near the end of the body. Ventral scales 189–241 (males), 197–232 (females); subcaudals 179–199 (males), 169–183 (females); upper labials 8–9, with the fourth to sixth touching the eye. Rich dark green on head and body, some snakes with obscure oblique, dark bands crossing the forward third of the body. The head is usually somewhat lighter than the body. The underside is light green, with a white line on each side near the end of the ventrals. Juveniles have short, oblique, bright blue markings on the sides of the neck and first half of the body.

The Green Vine Snake is common almost everywhere, from house  compounds, shrubby road margins, secondary growth and tree plantations, to primary rain forest. It occurs from near sea level to about 1200 m. It is active both by day and night. The diet consists mainly of lizards. The groove before the eye on the side of the snout makes it possible for this species and the preceding one to see straight forward and line up its prey with steroescopic vision. Although both species of *Ahaetulla* are rear-fanged snakes, their venom does not seem to affect people. They are not aggressive but have an interesting threat display in which they extend the tongue halfway and leave it extended as long as they feel disturbed.

Bjorn Lardner

(Opposite). *Ahaetulla prasina.*
(Left). Devouring a lizard.

Boiga
Cat Snakes

These medium- to large-sized snakes are nocturnal and have vertical cat-like pupils, accounting for their common name. All are rear-fanged ("opisthoglyphous") and venomous. The venom does not seem to be dangerous to people, however, and there are no reports of serious symptoms from bites. All cat-snakes have long teeth, especially *Boiga cynodon*, and they can make nasty cuts that bleed profusely. All species are nocturnal and at least partially arboreal. They feed on vertebrate prey, the larger species eating mainly birds and mammals and the smaller species mainly small mammals, lizards, and frogs.

Boiga cynodon
Dog-Toothed Cat Snake

Described originally from Sumatra, *Boiga cynodon* is widely distributed in South-east Asia, Sumatra, Borneo, Java, and as far east as Flores in the Lesser Sundas. It has been found in all parts of Borneo. *Cyno* = dog, and *don* = tooth, a reference to the very long teeth of this species.

Boiga cynodon is a large snake, frequently growing to more than two metres. The head is broad and much wider than the neck. The body is flattened from side to side because of the ridged back and has an almost triangular shape in cross-section. One of the most impressive features of this species is its extraordinarily long teeth, especially those at the front of the palate and lower jaw. One hopes not to see these in the living snake. The smooth scales are in 25 rows in the front part of the body, reducing to 23 at mid-body, and dropping to 15 just before the tail. The scales in the vertebral row are larger than adjacent scales. Ventral scales 281–290 (males), 278–290 (females); subcaudals 149–158 (males), 147–165 (females); upper labials 8–9, with fourth to sixth touching the eye.

The usual colour is fawn or tan, with narrow black cross bands in an X-like shape. The first quarter of the snake usually has a black stripe along the ridge of the back. The head has the same ground colour of the body, with a dark stripe from the eye to the rear of the head. The tail is black circled by narrow white rings. The belly has the same colour as the trunk and is

(Above and below). *Boiga cynodon.*

generally unmarked, while the throat is yellowish. Occasional individuals of this species are entirely dark brown.

Boiga cynodon is largely arboreal and lives in primary forest in both flat and hilly terrain, in secondary forests, and even in towns. It is rarely seen more than 500 metres above sea level. It patrols shrubs and trees overhanging small creeks and rivers searching for birds, its principal prey. We once found a 2.4 m dead specimen draped over branches above the Mengiong River; in its stomach was a very large pigeon. The extremely long teeth seem adapted to fast penetration through layers of feathers. Although *Boiga cynodon* is commonly seen along streams, and even swimming across quite wide rivers, it also moves freely through forests at some distance from water. When alarmed, it flattens its neck vertically, exposing the bright yellow throat.

Boiga dendrophila
Yellow-Ringed Cat Snake or Mangrove Snake

This species was described from specimens from Java, but occurs from southern Peninsular Malaysia, Sumatra, and Borneo to the Lesser Sunda Islands, Sulawesi, and the Philippines. It occurs throughout Borneo. *Dendron* = tree; and *philia* = affection. The name refers to the snake's arboreal habits.

This is a large snake, reaching a total length of near 2.5 metres. Individuals two metres long are common. The head is wider than the neck, with a relatively short snout and a large eye. The body is somewhat flattened from side to side with a ridged vertebral line. The tail is relatively short, accounting for 20–23% of the total length. There are 23 rows of smooth scales around the neck, 21 at mid-body, and 15 just before the tail. Ventral scales 224–240 (males), 240–247 (females); subcaudals 102–111 (males), 106–113 (females); upper labials eight, with third to sixth touching eye. This is a glossy black snake with narrow canary yellow rings. In the Bornean population the rings are one or two scales wide, about 40 to 50 before the tail and about 10 on the tail; the black intervals between yellow rings are 5 to 10 scales wide. The head is black above and on the upper part of the side. The upper lip is bright yellow with narrow black bars. The belly is black. Populations of this species from other areas may have wider or fewer yellow rings.

Boiga dendrophila is a snake of both primary and disturbed habitats of the lowland coastal and interior areas. Although abundant in mangrove (which gives it one of its common names), it is equally abundant far inland, from primary forest to agricultural scrub areas. It eats all kinds of small vertebrates—frogs, lizards, snakes, birds, and rodents. In captivity, a small (*ca.* 1 m) *Boiga dendrophila* from Pulau Tiga in Sabah ate frogs, mice and once attempted to eat a 1.5 m long Vine Snake (*Ahaetulla prasina*). The Yellow-Ringed Cat Snake lays from four to 15 eggs.

This species is a favourite of medicine sellers in Malaysia because, although it looks impressively dangerous, it tames rather easily. These are the same qualities, as well as its brilliant coloration, that make it a favorite of zoo curators. As an adult, it is unmistakable. Small snakes (less than one metre) are similar to juvenile cobras, which also have light rings. However, juvenile cobras have head and neck the same diameter and their light rings are broader, yellowish white. Juvenile king cobras have narrow yellow rings, but also have a yellow snout. The Banded Krait (p. 189) has whitish and black bands of equal width. Two species of Wolf Snakes (*Lycodon*) have light and dark rings as juveniles (less than one metre), but in *Lycodon subcinctus* the white bands are five scales wide (p. 101) and in *Lycodon albofuscus* the black areas do not cross the belly.

R.B. Stuebing

Boiga dendrophila.

121

Boiga drapiezii
Spotted Cat Snake

Originally described from Java, this species is now known from Peninsular Malaysia, Singapore, Sumatra, and Borneo. Although found at scattered localities in Sabah and Sarawak, there are still no records from Kalimantan, but it surely occurs there. The specific name probably refers to an early collector in the East Indies.

This is a long, slender snake with the head much wider than the thin neck and the body flattened from side to side. The front third or half of the body is remarkably thin and it is only the rear of the body that has any bulk to it. Maximum length is about two metres, with the tail making up 24–27%. The eye is large, about equal to the length of the snout. There are 19 rows of smooth scales to mid-body, reducing to 17 or 15 just before the tail. Scales in the vertebral row are larger than adjacent scales. Ventral scales 262–287 (males), 258–274 (females); subcaudals 150–173 (males), 151–157 (females); upper labials 8–9, with third to fifth or third to sixth touching the eye.

R.B. Stuebing

Boiga drapiezii.

122

R.B. Stuebing

Boiga drapiezii. Close-up of head.

Boiga drapiezi has complicated coloration. The ground colour is usually greenish-grey to orange-brown with small pinkish vertebral spots in pairs on the front third of the body, gradually fusing to form a thin light line running the rest of the length. The sides have a series of light and dark brown vertical bars or bands, the darkest of which shorten to roundish spots towards the rear of the body. Some snakes have narrow pink vertical bars. Most individuals have bright pink or white spots low on the sides and adjacent parts of the ventral scales. The top of the head usually has dark speckling, without a clear pattern. The belly is pinkish, heavily dusted with brown and usually with a thin dark line on each side near the outer ends of the ventrals.

Boiga drapiezi is a nocturnal snake of primary and secondary lowland forests, up to about 1000 metres. We have seen it most often in low vegetation, but assume that it also moves through the middle canopy. As it moves through the branches, it frequently extends its body stiffly forward for at least one-third of its length and could easily be mistaken for a vine. When held, it will typically extend itself straight up towards the face of its handler. People who are not fond of snakes find this habit rather ominous and unnerving. *Boiga drapiezi* feeds on frogs and arboreal lizards, even eating the gliding lizards, *Draco*. The diet may occasionally include a large insect. Eggs are said to be laid in the nests of tree termites, where from four to ten eggs are deposited.

Boiga jaspidea
Jasper Cat Snake

Java is the source for the first specimen. The species is also known from Peninsular Malaysia, Singapore, Sumatra, and Borneo. It appears to be widely distributed in Borneo. *Iaspis* = jasper, referring to the reddish brown colour.

Boiga jaspidea is a medium-sized slender snake strongly flattened from side to side. Maximum size is about 1.5 m, with the tail equalling 24–28% of the total. The head is much wider than the neck and the diameter of the eye equals the length of the snout. The smooth scales are in 21 rows to mid-body, reducing to 15 just before the tail. Scales of the vertebral row are larger than adjacent scales. Ventral scales 249–263 (males), 243–252 (females); subcaudals 146–159 (males), 140–143 (females); upper labials eight, with third to fifth touching the eye.

The general colour is reddish brown with several rows of dark brown or black checks down the centre of the back and along the sides. Often the rear

R.F. Inger

Boiga jaspidea.

124

Boiga jaspidea.

of the back has whitish squares alternating with dark spots. A row of white rectangles is usually present low on the sides. The belly is heavily dusted with brown, without a pattern. Except in occasional individuals, the top of the head has fine speckling and several light-edged black spots. One of these dark spots on the centre of the head begins just behind the level of the eyes and continues as a black stripe for a short distance down the neck.

Boiga jaspidea lives in primary and secondary forests from near sea level to about 1000 metres. It has been observed moving through shrubs and low (up to 5 metres) in trees and occasionally on the ground. It is capable, like *Boiga drapiezi*, of extending the front third or so of its body straight out horizontally. Presumably its diet is similar to that of *B. drapiezi*. One specimen was found with a tree mouse in its stomach and another had eaten a small snake. It is said to deposit its eggs in termite nests above ground, where about six eggs are deposited.

Boiga jaspidea and *Boiga drapiezii* are alike in general shape and size. But *jaspidea* never has the dark lines on the belly found in *drapiezii* and *drapiezii* never has the dark pattern on the head found in *jaspidea*.

125

Boiga nigriceps
Dark-Headed Cat Snake

Described from an unspecificied locality in the "East Indies," *Boiga nigriceps* occurs in Peninsular Malaysia, Sumatra and adjacent small islands, Borneo, and Java. It has been found in Sabah and Sarawak, but there are no reports from Kalimantan or Brunei yet. *Nigra* = dark; and *ceps* = head.

Boiga nigriceps is a medium-sized snake reaching a maximum between 1.5 and 2 metres, with the tail equalling about 25% of the total length. Its body is flattened from side to side as in most Cat Snakes, but it is not as

Boiga nigriceps.

Ralph Cutter

126

slender as *Boiga drapiezi* or *B. jaspidea*. The head is much wider than the neck and the eye is large. The smooth scales are in 21 rows at mid-body, reducing to 15 before the tail. Scales in the vertebral row are much larger than adjacent scales. Ventral scales 262–2693 (males), 246–260 (females); subcaudals 143 (males), 137–148 (females); upper labials eight, with third to fifth touching the eye. This is a brown or olive-brown snake without distinctive pattern. The head and often the tail are darker than the body. The lips and underside of the head are white or, sometimes, yellowish. On each side of the back there are small dark dots that form a line running most of the length of the body. Larger snakes may lack this pattern. The belly is white, becoming brownish in the rear part of the body.

Not much is known about the habits of this species, although it is likely to be arboreal. Most records are from primary forest in flat and hilly terrain at low elevations. There are few observations on the diet, but one *Boiga nigriceps* that we examined had eaten a medium-sized snake (*ca.* 40 cm) and another contained a few feathers. There has been a report of a venomous bite by this snake, but there are no such records from Borneo.

Calamaria
Reed Snakes

It is easy to identify a snake as belonging to this genus. All are small, usually about the size of a long pencil. All have a small head, no wider than the body. All have small eyes. All have very short tails that taper only near the tip. Finally, all have certain groups of head scales fused: the internasals are fused with the prefrontals (see Fig. 4E on p. 53).

Identification to genus is the easy part. Identification to species is difficult, very difficult even for snake experts. Part of the problem is caused by the large number of species—21, making this the largest genus of snakes in Borneo. But the real difficulty is caused by the subtlety of patterns of variation. In some species juveniles have one colour pattern, adults another. In other species, there is variation among the adults. In some species, adults vary in the amount of yellow on the head; in others, that kind of variation separates juveniles from adults. In certain cases, one species differs from another in the number of ventral scales; for example, males of *Calamaria suluensis* have fewer than 145 ventrals, whereas males of *C. grabowskyi* have more than 145.

Small species of snakes, total length to 690 mm, usually less than 275 mm; head not wider than body, neck not narrowed, body with uniform diameter (unless female contains eggs); tail short, blunt or tapered near tip; internasals and prefrontals fused (see diagram); four or five upper labial scales; ventral scales 135–305, caudal scales 8–32. Coloration varies widely. The side and back may be uniform dark brown or black, black with narrow light stripes on the centres of scale rows, black with yellow rings, light tan or grey with a dark network on each scale, or greyish with narrow black stripes. The belly and under side of the head may be white, cream-coloured with black spots of varying size, pink, or red.

All species of *Calamaria* are secretive, hiding by day under logs, rocks, and dead leaves. At night, they apparently wander through the leaf litter searching for their single type of prey—earthworms. Although there is little firm information, some species may move quite far during the night. One species, *Calamaria griswoldi*, has been found frequently dead on roads around the Headquarters of Kinabalu Park. In some areas *Calamaria* seem to be relatively abundant, or at least easy to discover by turning rotting logs. But in most places, one rarely sees them no matter how many rotting logs are rolled over. When removed from their retreats, these snakes sometimes use a peculiar form of sidewinding locomotion in trying to escape. With the head held to the ground, the snake may raise a loop of the body above the ground and throw it forward. Repeating this motion rapidly, the snake is appears to be rolling or tumbling forward and moving with much greater speed than usual. Another defensive tactic of these snakes when gripped firmly is to push the tip of the stubby tail, which is sharply pointed in many species, against the hand holding it. All species of *Calamaria* lay eggs in litter on the forest floor. Clutch sizes are small, numbering two to four eggs that are 20–35 mm long and 7–9 mm in diameter.

Calamaria = reed, presumably referring to the non-tapered shape.

Calamaria grabowskyi
Grabowsky's Reed Snake

Found in Telang and Tamianglajang, Dusson Timor District, Kalimantan, and widespread in Borneo, but not known from elsewhere. *Grabowskyi* = Fritz Grabowsky who explored the south-east corner of Kalimantan in 1880–1884 and collected the type specimen.

A small, slender snake, maximum size about 450 mm. Tail short, about one-tenth of body length. Scales smooth, in 13 rows entire length of body. Ventrals 150–186 (males), 164–190 (females); subcaudals 23–29 (males), 20–28 (females). Upper labials 5, third and fourth bordering eye. Medium to dark brown above, with small darker spots on head and scattered over body. Each dorsal scale has a fine dark network. The brown coloration ends at the third scale row in the front fifth of the body, but beyond that point covers the second row as well. The scales of the first row have large yellow centres, forming a black-edged yellow stripe. The upper lip and the ventral scales are yellow, with each ventral having a dark brown or black band across its front third. This gives the belly a distinctly banded pattern.

Calamaria suluensis and *C. everetti* have colour patterns very similar to that of *C. grabowskyi*, but both of the first two have yellow ventrals with dark pigment confined to the corners or to dots running down the centre of the belly. There are also differences in the number of ventral scales.

This is a forest species that ranges from the lowlands up to 1430 metres above sea level.

Calamaria grabowskyi.

129

Calamaria griswoldi
Lined Reed Snake

This species was described from Bundu Tuhan, Mount Kinabalu, Sabah, and almost all known records are from the environs of Mount Kinabalu, above 1200 metres above sea level. There is one record from the Kelabit Plateau in Sarawak, presumably at or above 1000 metres. *Griswoldi* = J.A. Griswold, Jr., the discoverer of this species.

A small snake, though large for the genus, maximum length to 488 mm. Body slender, tail short, less than one-tenth of the total length. Scales smooth, in 13 rows entire length of body. Ventrals 155–179 (males), 183–192 (females); subcaudals 16–18 (males), 13–16 (females); upper labials 5, third and fourth bordering eye. This species is black above and on the sides, with very narrow white lines on the edges of all scale rows above the first. The upper lip and the entire underside are cream-coloured. The first scale row is also cream-coloured. In some individuals there is a faint zigzag black line down the centre of the belly and tail.

This is the only Bornean species of *Calamaria* with light lines on the edges of scale rows.

It lives in submontane and montane forests. Many specimens have been found dead on the road at the headquarters of Kinabalu Park, indicating that the species wanders quite a bit during the night.

Calamaria leucogaster
Collared Reed Snake

The type specimen is from Ampat Lawang, Sumatra, but the species is widespread in Borneo. *Leuco* = white, *gaster* = belly, referring to the light underside.

A small snake, maximum known length 223 mm. Body rather stout and snout narrow for the genus. Tail tapering to a sharp point, usually less than one-tenth of total length. Scales smooth, in 13 rows entire length of body. Ventrals 126–146 (males), 129–157 (females); subcaudals 17–26 (males), 12–19 (females); upper labials 5, third and fourth bordering eye. These are pinkish brown snakes, each scale having a dark network on a light brown background. The head is brown with a yellow lip and a narrow yellow streak from the snout passing above the eye and widening slightly at the rear of the head. A black half ring around the neck (the "collar") two to three scales wide. Two similar black half-rings at the end of the snake, a wide one at the base of the tail and a narrow one at the tip of the tail. Between the two black rings, the tail is a deep salmon-pink, almost red. The entire underside is yellow.

This is the only Bornean species of *Calamaria* with black half-rings on the neck and tail. In fact, no other Bornean snake has this pattern.

The Collared Reed Snake lives in lowland rain forest. Like all species of this genus, it feeds on earthworms and lives in the leaf litter of the forest floor.

Calamaria lowi
Low's Reed Snake

The type locality is the Rejang River, Sarawak. The species is widespread in Sarawak and Kalimantan, but known so far only from the western part of Sabah. Different races of this species occur in Peninsular Malaysia and Java. *Lowi* = named for Hugh Low, former Governor of Labuan, who discovered this and other Bornean species of reptiles and amphibians.

An extremely slender species of *Calamaria*, with a very small head and tiny eye. The longest known specimen is 315 mm. The tail is short, thick, and slightly tapered at the end. Scales smooth, in 13 rows entire length of the body. Ventrals 190–222 (males), 218–254 (females); subcaudals 17–26 (males), 11–18 (females); upper labials 4, the second and third bordering the eye. Head and body are dark grey to brown. The upper lip is lemon yellow. There is a yellow spot on the side of the neck, usually followed by two similar spots on the front of the body. The tail has two yellow spots, a larger one on the side of the body at the base of the tail and a smaller one at the tip. There are three general patterns. Some individuals have two or three narrow light stripes on each side and a row of widely spaced, small yellow spots running down the centre of the back. Others have the light stripes but no spots on the back. Both of these types have the entire underside of the body dark grey or brown. A third type lacks the light stripes, but has 20–35 yellow spots low on the side and extending onto the grey or brown belly.

This species is not likely to be confused with any other. Its extremely slender body, small head, and tiny eye are very distinctive.

It occurs in flat and hilly terrain at low elevations, burrowing in soil or living under dead leaves. Although it lives in rainforest, it also has been found in pepper gardens. This and other secretive snakes are sometimes washed out of their retreats on the forest floor into rivers by very heavy rains.

Calamaria lumbricoidea
Variable Reed Snake

This species is known from Java, and widespread in Borneo. It also occurs in Peninsular Malaysia, Sumatra, and the Philippine Islands. *Lumbric* = earthworm, *oidea* = resembling, referring to earthworm-like shape.

A small snake, though the largest of the Reed Snakes, reaching 50 cm. Tail short, at most about one-eighth of total length. Scales smooth, in 13 rows entire length of body. Ventrals 145–181 (males), 137–199 (females); subcaudals 19–26 (males), 14–21 (females); upper labials 5, third and fourth bordering eye. Juveniles have red heads and necks and black bodies with narrow whitish or yellow rings. This pattern holds until the snake reaches

R.F. Inger

Calamaria lumbricoidea.

132

about 200 mm. Then the head begins to acquire black pigment, starting with the snout. By the time the snake reaches 300 mm and is adult, black pigment has displaced all of the red. The light rings also narrow as the snake grows and disappear completely by the time the snake reaches 300 mm. The underside is yellow with groups of 2–4 black ventrals spaced at regular intervals. At the front third of the body, the lowest two rows of scales are yellow, forming a stripe separating the black upper parts from the groups of black ventrals.

The red-headed juveniles are superficially like juvenile coral snakes (genus *Maticora*), very small Kraits (*Bungarus*), and Pipe Snakes (*Cylindrophis*). None of these species has the narrow light rings that circle the body of young *C. lumbricoidea*. Other species of *Calamaria* have black on the ventrals, but the only other species (*C. borneensis*) that sometimes has pairs of black ventrals has only four upper labials.

This is mainly a forest species, but may also occur in degraded, secondary growth forest or shady gardens.

Calamaria suluensis
Yellow-bellied Reed Snake

Originally described from Cagayan Sulu, Philippine Islands, the species is known from Kalimantan, Sabah, and Sarawak. *Suluensis* = from the Sulu Islands.

A small, slender snake, maximum size about 300 mm. Tail short, about one-tenth of body length. Scales smooth, in 13 rows entire length of body. Ventrals 131–138 (males), 144–161 (females); subcaudals 18–20 (males), 15–20 (females). Upper labials 5, third and fourth bordering eye. Medium to dark brown above, with small darker spots on head and scattered over body. Each dorsal scale has a fine dark network. Scales of first row with yellow centres froming a light stripe running most of the distance to the tail. The upper lip and the ventral scales are yellow. In some individuals, the ventrals have a small dark spot on the midline forming a dotted line.

Similar in coloration to *C. grabowskyi* (see p. 128), but differing in lacking dark bands across the ventral scales and in having fewer ventral scales.

All snakes of this species we have seen were on the floor in primary forest under dead leaves or 1–2 cm under soil. The species occurs from near sea level to 1430 metres.

Chrysopelea paradisi
Paradise Tree Snake

Java is the type locality, but this species is widely distributed in Peninsular Malaysia, Sumatra and the islands off its west coast, Borneo, and the Philippine Islands. It has been found at many places in Sabah and Sarawak and probably occurs throughout the island. *Chrysos*, Greek, meaning gold; *pileos* (?), Greek, meaning "cap", although this definition is uncertain. *Paradisus* in Latin means paradise, presumably a reference to the beautiful coloration.

This is a slender snake with a long head wider than the neck, and a tail about 25% of total length. Maximum size is about 1.5 m. The snout is long, flat, and rounded at the end. The eye is large and bulges out to the side; its diameter equals the distance between the eye and the nostril. The smooth scales are in 17 rows at mid-body, but reduced to 13 before the tail. The scales of the three rows along the centre of the back and in the row next to the ventrals are larger than rest. Both the ventrals and the caudals have a sharp keel near the outer edges. Ventral scales 224–239 (males), 218–233

R.B. Stuebing

Chrysopelea paradisi.

134

(females); subcaudals 118–137 (males), 122–136 (females); upper labials 9, sometimes 8, with the fifth and sixth touching the eye. The head and body are black, with a bright green spot in the centre of all scales on the sides of the body. Down the centre of the back is a row of three- or four-petalled pink or red spots. The scales on the top of the head have many small yellow-green spots that fuse to form transverse lines crossing the head just in front of and just behind the eyes and at the rear of the head. The lips and underside of the head are yellow-green. The belly and underside of the tail are green, with each scale outlined in black.

This strictly arboreal species seems to be equally at home in primary and secondary forests, mainly at low elevations. It appears in tree-shaded gardens and even has been found in the attics of old houses. The diet consists of small lizards, mostly geckos. The Paradise Tree Snake can glide by launching itself from branches after contracting the belly to form a concave surface.

This species and *Chrysopelea pelias* are rear-fanged, but the venom does not appear to affect humans. Michael Tweedie, author of *The Snakes of Malaya*, said he was bitten several times without any symptoms, and one of us (RBS) has had the same experience.

Chrysopelea pelias
Twin-Barred Tree Snake

The type locality is uncertain, but the species is known from Peninsular Malaysia, Singapore, Sumatra and the islands off the west coast, Borneo, and Java. It has been seen across Sabah and in widely spaced places in Sarawak. It probably also occurs in Kalimantan and Brunei. *Pelias* = cap (?).

This species is a medium-sized, slender snake, with head wider than the neck and the tail one-fourth of total length. The eye is relatively large, but does not protrude as does the eye of the related Paradise Tree Snake. The ventrals and subcaudals have a sharp keel near the outer edges. The scales are smooth in 17 rows at mid-body, but reducing to 13 rows near the end of the body. All the scales are about equal. Ventral scales 181–199; subcaudals 111–120; upper labials 9, with fourth to sixth bordering the eye. The centre of the back has red rectangles separated by pairs of narrow black bars, each pair split by a light brown or yellowish bar. The black bars may cross the entire side. The side below the red and black pattern is brownish. The top of the head is brown, crossed by three narrow red bars, in front of the eyes, behind the eyes, and at the rear of the head. There are also yellowish or light brown irregular spots on the head shields. The upper lip is yellowish with dark spots on each labial scale. The belly is dark brown or black, sometimes with yellowish spots at the outer edges of the ventral scales.

This species lives in primary forest from near sea level to 600 metres. The diet consists of lizards.

Yong Hoi Sen

Chrysopelea pelias.

Dendrelaphis caudolineatus
Striped Bronze-Back

It is not known exactly where the type specimen came from, but the species ranges from Peninsular Malaysia through the East Indies as far as Halmahera and the Philippines. It occurs throughout Borneo. *Dendron* = tree, and *elaphis* = a kind of snake; *cauda* = tail, and *linea* = line, referring to the pattern.

This is a medium-sized, slender snake with a long tail. Maximum length is about 1.5 m, with the tail accounting for a bit more than one-fourth. The tail is whip-like and, unlike that of most snakes, tends to break near the tip. The head is wider than the neck, with a bluntly rounded snout and a rather large eye. The smooth scales are in 13 rows, reducing to 11 near the tail. Both

136

Dendrelaphis caudolineatus.

C.L. Chan

the ventrals and subcaudals have a sharp keel near their outer ends. Ventral scales 173–189 (males), 174–186 (females); subcaudals 105–116 (males), 110–112 (females); upper labials 9, the fifth and sixth bordering the eye. The top of the head and body are olive brown, with a pale green stripe low on the side flanked above by a narrow black line and below by a wider black stripe. Towards the rear of the body, thin black stripes develop on the back and all of these, plus the ones low on the side, become very conspicuous on the tail. The lip and underside of the head and body are pale green.

Dendrelaphis caudolineatus lives in primary and secondary forest and will also move along the edges of clearings or in shaded gardens. It is an accomplished climber, but is often seen on the ground hunting its prey during the day. It feeds on lizards and frogs, but is especially adept at catching skinks of the genus *Mabuya*, which bask in patches of sunlight. This is one of the mostly commonly seen snakes in Borneo.

All three Bornean species of the genus are similar in size, slender build, bronzy colour, and active, diurnal habits. Only *Dendelaphis caudolineatus* and *D. pictus* have black and light stripes low on the side and only *D. caudolineatus* has a striped tail.

Dendrelaphis caudolineatus.

Dendrelaphis formosus
Elegant Bronze-Back

The species was originally found in Java, but is known to occur from southern Thailand through Java and all the intervening islands. It is widely distributed in Borneo. The species name is taken from the Latin word, *formosus*, meaning beautiful, referring to the coloration.

A medium-sized, slender snake, with a long, whip-like tail. Maximum length is less than 1.5 m. The body is slightly flattened from side to side. The

Dendrelaphis formosus and (inset). Close-up of head by Bjorn Lardner.

139

head is wider than the neck and has a rather long, almost truncate snout. The eye is large, its diameter greater than the distance to the nostril. The smooth scales are in 15 rows until mid-body, after which they reduce to 11 rows just before the tail. The scales of the vertebral row are distinctly larger than adjacent scales. Both the ventrals and subcaudals have a sharp keel along their outer edges. Ventral scales 157–160 (males), 173–191 (females); subcaudals 149–152 (males), 140–149 (females); upper labials 9, with the fifth and sixth touching the eye. The top of the head and the central stripe along the back are olive brown. Each scale on the side has a light green centre and a narrow black edge, giving the side a series of pale green and narrow black, vertical bars. A black stripe runs from the side of the snout, through the eye, and ends at the rear of the head. The lip and the entire underside are light green.

This species lives in primary and secondary forests at low elevations. Like the preceding species, it feeds mainly on lizards. Although this is not a rare snake, few observations have been made on its habits. The body form and structure are those of arboreal snakes and the kinds of lizards we have found in stomachs indicate arboreal feeding. Six to eight eggs are laid.

Dendrelaphis pictus
Painted Bronze-Back

The type specimen came from either Java or Borneo, but the species is known throughout South-east Asia, through the larger islands and the Lesser Sundas, as far as Ambon and north to the Philippines. It occurs throughout Borneo. *Pictus* = painted, probably in reference to conspicuous coloration.

Dendelaphis pictus is a medium-sized snake reaching slightly more than 1.5 m. The tail is long, making up one-third of the total length. The head is wider than the neck, with a rounded snout. The eye, though large, is smaller than in the preceding species, being smaller than its distance to the nostril. The smooth scales are in 15 rows in the first third or so of the body and then begin to reduce in number until there are only 11 rows near the tail. Scales in the first (lowest) and vertebral rows are distinctly larger than scales of the intervening rows, until near the end of the body where the scales are roughly equal in size. Ventral and subcaudal scales are keeled at the sides. Ventral scales 170–187 (males), 169–194 (females); subcaudals 138–147 (males), 130–151 (females); upper labials 9, the fourth to sixth or fifth to sixth touching the eye. The top of the head and middle of the back are olive brown. A black stripe begins on the side of the snout, passes through the eye, and continues as a wide, diffuse band along the side of the body. In the first third of the body, this band has small light green spots arranged in vertical series. Farther back, the black narrows into a thin stripe. Below this dark streak is a light green stripe continuous from the neck to the end of the body. This stripe, in turn, is bordered below by a black stripe beginning just behind the neck and this stripe also stops at the end of the body. The tail is essentially not striped. The lower parts are light green.

This arboreal species lives in forests, secondary growth, and even in small towns at low elevations. It is very common in places, or at least seems so because it is an active species during the day and likely to be seen. It feeds mainly on tree frogs, but also takes lizards.

R.B. Stuebing

Dendrelaphis pictus.

Dryocalamus tristrigatus
Three-Lined Tree Snake

The type locality is unknown, but as the species is known only from Borneo and the Natuna Islands, the type specimen probably came from Borneo. *Dryos* = tree, *calamus* = reed, probably referring to both shape and habitat; *tri* = three, *striga* = row of hay, referring to the pattern.

A small, slender snake, maximum length about 700 mm, with the tail about one-fourth of the total length. The head is swollen just behind the eyes and abruptly narrows in front of the eyes to a rounded, somewhat flattened

Dryocalamus tristrigatus.

142

R.B. Stuebing

Dryocalamus tristrigatus. Close-up of head.

snout. The pupils of the eyes are vertically oval, and because of the narrowing of the head the eyes almost point directly forward. Like some of the wolf snakes (genus *Lycodon*), the loreal scale is long and borders the eye; there is usually no preocular scale. The scales of the body are smooth and in 15 rows. The ventrals are 209–235, and the subcaudals 87–99. The anal plate is not divided. The ventrals have a weak lateral (side) keel. This is a striped snake with a straw-coloured belly. The first scale row is pale yellow; rows two and three are chocolate brown; rows four and part of five are pale yellow; the rest of row five, all of row six, and most of row seven are brown; the upper edge of row seven and all of the vertebral row are pale yellow. All stripes are continuous from the rear of the neck to the end of the body. So above the lowest dark stripes, there are three pale yellow (or hay-coloured) stripes. The belly is pale yellow, usually with a dark dot at the side ends of each ventral scale. The head and neck are dark brown above and on the sides. The upper lip is yellow and each scale on the top and side of the head is edged in yellow.

The only Bornean species that might possibly be confused with this one is *Liopeltis longicauda* but in that species the light stripes run only about half way down the body.

This forest species lives in a variety of terrain, from flat, peaty areas to steep hilly forests. It has been found on the ground as well as in trees and shrubs, one to three metres above ground. These few observations probably do not give us the true range of microhabitats for this species because it can climb up tree trunks and may spend considerable time high in the canopy. There is no information on diet.

Dryocalamus subannulatus
Brown-Saddled Tree Snake

This species was described originally from western Sumatra, but is known also from Peninsular Malaysia, Singapore, the small islands off the west coast of Sumatra, and Borneo. The only Bornean record we know of is of a snake found at the outskirts of Sandakan. *Sub* = somewhat, *annulatus* = ringed, referring to the pattern.

A small slender tree snake rarely exceeding 50 cm, with the tail accounting for about one-fifth of the total. It is very similar to the Three-Lined Tree Snake (*Dryocalamus tristrigatus*) in general form. The head is swollen behind the eyes and tapers to a rather narrow snout. The eye has vertically oval pupils, and the loreal scale contacts the eye. The scales are smooth in 15 rows. A weak keel runs along the outer ends of the ventral scales. Ventral scales number 225–244; the anal plate is undivided. Subcaudals 88–107; upper labials seven, the third and fourth touching the eye.

This is a pale tan and dark brown banded snake. The dark bands, about three scales wide and beginning on the second scale row, occupy most of the area and are separated by narrow light spaces only one or two scales wide. The head scales are dark brown, edged or crossed by narrow light yellow-brown lines. The entire underside is yellow.

This species has been observed so rarely that nothing is known of its habits.

Dryophiops rubescens
Keel-Bellied Vine Snake

There was some doubt about the exact origin of the type specimen, but it was thought to be from the Malay Peninsula. It is now known from Peninsular Malaysia, Singapore, Sumatra, and Java. It has been observed on both coasts of Sabah, at Mount Mulu in Sarawak, and in south-eastern Kalimantan. *Drys* = tree, *ophis* = snake, *ops* = like, probably referring to the similarity to *Ahaetulla*. *Rubescens*= reddish, referring to the colour.

A slender, medium-sized snake reaching a maximum length of just over one metre. The tail is long and thin and forms about 30% of the total. The elongate head is considerably wider than the neck, but distinctly flattened. The snout is much longer than the diameter of the large eye. The pupil is horizontal, but not as extreme as in *Ahaetulla*. As in the case of the Banded and Green Vine Snakes, there is a groove along the side of the snout in front of the eye. The ventral scales have a distinct keel and notch near their outer ends. The smooth scales are arranged in 15 rows, reducing to 11 in the rear half of the body. Ventral scales 191–192 (males), 188–199 (females); subcaudals 119–125 (males), 111–119 (females); anal divided; upper labials nine, with fourth to sixth touching the eye. Light greyish to reddish brown, usually with small dark spots down the centre of the back and similar spots on the sides. The top of the head is pale brown with dark brown streaks. The side of the head has a dark stripe from near the tip of the snout, through the eye to the rear of the head. The lip is white with a few small dark spots. The ventral coloration is white under the head and neck, gradually darkening and becoming dark greyish brown for most of the length.

All records of this snake are from low elevations. We have seen it in secondary growth and on shrubs in gardens. Presumably, it also lives in primary forest. One specimen had eaten a flying lizard (*Draco*). Presumably, lizards are the main item in the diet.

In general form and coloration this species can be mistaken for the Banded Vine Snake (*Ahaetulla fasciolata*). But *Dryophiops* is easily distinguished from the Banded Vine Snake by its keeled ventrals, a feature absent in the other vine snakes.

Bjorn Lardner

Dryophiops rubescens.

Elaphe, Gonyophis, Gonyosoma

These three genera are related groups of medium-sized to large snakes referred to as "rat snakes" or "racers" in English language texts. Although some in our region have dull coloration, two are brightly coloured, and one of these (*Gonyophis margaritatus*) is perhaps the most beautiful snake in Borneo. The head is barely wider than the neck, slightly flattened and tapered, and the snout is relatively blunt. The teeth are not large and are uniform in size and shape. They have smooth or keeled scales and a rather distinct, almost sharp edge at the outer portion of the ventral scales. They are at least partially arboreal and feed on rodents (hence one of the common names) and birds which they sometimes take out of nests. In the case of *Elaphe taeniura*, climbing is done in caves, in search of bats. All are constrictors, quickly suffocating a prey animal by enveloping it in tight coils of the body. Both *Gonyophis* and *Gonyosoma* have convincing threat displays, flattening the neck, which leads some people to assume the snakes are venomous. Some *Elaphe* raise the head and vibrate the tail when alarmed. None of these snakes is poisonous but they will bite.

Elaphe flavolineata
Common Racer

Originally described from Java, this snake occurs from southern Thailand to Java and Sumatra. It is widespread in Borneo and has been reported from many places in Kalimantan, Sabah, and Sarawak. *Elaphe* may be derived from *elaps* a kind of snake; *flavo* = yellow, *lineatus* = of a line, referring to the yellow vertebral stripe in young snakes of this species.

It is a medium-sized snake, reaching 1.8 m in total length. The tail length is moderate, about 25% of the total or less. The snout is relatively long, equalling about twice the eye diameter. The scales are keeled, except for the lowest two rows. There are 19 rows of scales at mid-body. The anal scale is undivided. Ventral scales 205–218 (males), 215–233 (females); subcaudals 94–108 (males), 91–100 (females); anal undivided; upper labials usually 8, sometimes 9, the fourth to sixth touching the eye. Dark brown or blackish, darker towards the rear. Juveniles have a distinctly striped pattern, with a pair of black stripes separated by a yellowish stripe down the centre of the back;

occasional individuals have light blue patches on the sides of the neck. The stripes fade out in the the rear half of the body and usually disappear as the snake ages. Usually there are dark blotches low on the side. The head is brown above and the lips and chin white. A vertical black bar runs from the eye to the mouth and an oblique black streak runs from the eye to the angle of the jaws.

The Common Racer is widespread in the lowlands of Borneo, up to an elevation of 1000 metres. It is often found dead on roads near villages, towns, and agricultural areas. The diet consists mainly of rats and other small vertebrates.

Two other species of *Elaphe* have been reported from Borneo once or twice. One of them, *Elaphe radiata*, the Copperhead Racer, resembles *E. flavolineata* in having 19 scale rows at mid-body and an undivided anal scale, but differs in head pattern. *Elaphe radiata* has a thin vertical black line from the eye to the lip, a thin oblique black line from the eye to the angle of the mouth, and a wider horizontal black line from the eye to the rear of the head where it joins a black half ring circling the head. The second uncommon racer is *Elaphe erythrura*, the Philippine Red-tailed Racer. This species resembles *E. flavolineata* and *E. radiata* in having an undivided anal scale, but has no markings on the head or body and has a red tail; it also differs from the other Bornean racer, *E. taeniura*, in lacking a striped tail. *Elaphe erythrura* is very common in the Philippines and *Elaphe radiata* in Peninsular Malaysia; why these two species should be so uncommon in Borneo is unclear.

R.B. Stuebing

Elaphe flavolineata.

147

Elaphe taeniura
Cave Racer

The type specimens of this species came from eastern China and Thailand, but the species is very widely distributed from China and northeastern India, throughout South-east Asia, to Borneo and Sumatra. In Borneo it is known so far only from a few places in western Sabah and northern Sarawak, but probably is much more widespread. *Taenia* = ribbon, *ura* = tail, referring to the striped tail.

Elaphe taeniura.

Au Kam Wah

Elaphe taeniura.

A medium-sized to large snake, reaching 2 m in length. The tail is relatively short, 17–20% of total length. The snout is long, about two and a half times the diameter of the eye. The scales are smooth, except for the uppermost rows, and usually in 25 rows at mid-body. The anal scale is divided. Ventral scales 271–294 (males), 285–293 (females); subcaudals 94–101 (males), 86–95 (females); anal divided; upper labials 8 or 9, fifth and sixth (usually) or fourth to sixth touching the eye. Greyish brown or dark brown, usually with an indistinct, thin, chain-like pattern behind the neck. Near the middle of the body the coloration changes into a pattern of two broad, brown stripes on the sides separated by a white stripe down the centre of the back and bordered low on the side by another white stripe. The striped pattern is particularly bright on the tail. The top of the head and neck are olive, the lips and chin white, the two colours separated by a black streak beginning on the snout, passing through the eye, and ending at the rear of the head. The belly is yellowish or whitish.

The Cave Racer has been found in Borneo from near sea level to about 2000 m. The species is most frequently encountered in caves, where it takes up residence to feed on roosting bats. It is not aggressive, but will bite if handled. The Cave Racer appears much less likely to be found near human activities than the Common Racer.

Gonyophis margaritatus
Royal Tree Snake

The type locality is "Sarawak," and the species is known from a number of places in the state. It has also been found at several localities in Sabah and one in Kalimantan, and probably occurs throughout Borneo, though it is nowhere common. It is also known from Peninsular Malaysia. *Gonyo* = angled, and *ophis* = snake; the name refers to the keeled ventral and subcaudal scales. *Margaritatus* = adorned with pearls, surely referring to the spots in the centres of the body scales.

A medium-sized, rather slender snake, with maximum length less than 2 m and the tail accounting for about 22% of the total. The head is long, is slightly wider than the neck, and has a blunt snout. The body is slightly flattened from side to side. The upper rows of body scales are weakly keeled. There are 19 rows of scales at mid-body, reducing to 17 or 15 just before the tail. The ventrals and subcaudals have a distinct keel along their outer edges. Ventrals 234–242 (females); subcaudals 108–121; anal divided; upper labials 9, fourth to sixth bordering the eye.

The general colour is dark, speckled with turquoise and, in the rear half, ringed with yellow-orange bands. The front part of the head including the snout, upper and lower labials, chin, and underside of the neck are deep

R.B. Stuebing

(Opposite). *Gonyophis margaritatus*. (Above). Close-up of head.

golden yellow. The eyes are reddish to dark brown. The side of the head has a wide dark band running back from the eye; each scale in the band is black with a turquoise centre. The scales of the body are glossy black, each with a light centre. These light spots are turquoise in the front part of the body gradually changing to deep yellow and then deep orange. The light centres become larger and towards the rear of the body form orange rings that partially encircle the snake. Each orange ring is about three scales wide. The tail is completely encircled by orange and black rings. The ventral scales are yellow (in the front part of the body) and orange (to the rear), margined with a thin black edge.

Gonyophis margaritatus is an arboreal snake living in rain forests at low elevations (below 700 m). Like a number of arboreal Bornean snakes, this species is able to climb straight up the trunks of trees that have apparently smooth bark. A captive specimen refused all food except fish.

R.B. Stuebing

Gonyosoma oxycephalum
Grey-Tailed Racer

(This species is called the Red-Tailed Racer in Peninsular Malaysia, but the many we have seen from Borneo have grey tails.)

The name for this species was based on snakes from Java, but it occurs from there to northern Thailand and southern Indochina, and throughout Borneo. *Gonio* = angled, and *soma* = body, referring to the sharp angle near the ends of the ventral scales. *Oxy* = sharp, and *cephalum* = head, referring to the rather tapered snout.

The Grey-Tailed Racer is a medium-sized to large snake, reaching 2 m or more. The tail is moderate, being 23–26% of the total. The head is barely wider than the neck, slightly flattened, and tapered. The long snout is about three times the length of the diameter of the eye. The ventral scales have a sharp angle near the outer ends. The scales of the back are smooth or feebly keeled. There are 23 or 25 rows at mid-body. The anal scale is divided. Ventral scales 229–243 (males), 242–255 (females); subcaudals 127–149 (males), 126–142 (females); anal divided; upper labials 7–10, usually 8 or 9, with the fifth and sixth or sixth and seventh touching the eye.

The top of the head is greenish yellow, while the upper surfaces of the body are bright green. Some of the scales are edged with yellow. Beyond mid-body, the yellow-edged scales increase, to form an indistinct pattern of diagonal stripes along the sides of the body. The belly is bright yellow. The tail is grey. The colour pattern with bright green body, yellow belly, and grey tail make this one of the easiest snakes to recognize in Borneo.

W.M. Poon

(Opposite). *Gonyosoma oxycephalum* and (above). Close-up of head.

J. Omar

The Grey-Tailed Racer is common throughout the lowlands of Borneo, up to about 1000 metres, and has been found on some small islands, such as Pulau Tiga and Pulau Gaya. It seems to prefer edge habitats and secondary growth, even entering gardens, where it feeds on small mammals and birds. The Dusun name for this snake, *masak punti* (ripening banana) reflects both its colour and its frequent occurrence in the disturbed areas where bananas grow. *Gonyosoma oxycephalum* lays from five to twelve eggs. The species has an interesting threat display, in which the neck is flattened top to bottom, and the bright blue-striped tongue extended and retracted in an extremely slow, deliberate fashion.

Liopeltis

All three Bornean species are small, relatively slender snakes. They are inhabitants of the floor of lowland forests. Two of the species are known to feed on spiders and other small invertebrates. The generic name is from *lio* = smooth, and *peltis* = shield, referring to the smooth scales.

1. A dark-edged, white, V-shaped marking on the nape. (Occasionally not present. See species description) .... *Liopeltis longicauda*

2. Upper labial scales white with black edges .... *Liopeltis baliodeirus*

3. Upper labial scales white without black edges .... *Liopeltis tricolor*

Liopeltis baliodeirus
Spotted Ground Snake

Originally described from Java, this species has been found in Sumatra and Peninsular Malaysia, as well as Borneo. It has been observed in forested areas throughout Sabah and Sarawak, and although it has been recorded from only one site in Kalimantan, it probably occurs widely in that state also. *Balios* = spotted, *deiro* = double, referring to the two rows of light spots on the fore part of the body.

R.B. Stuebing

R.B. Stuebing

(Above). *Liopeltis baliodeirus* and (below). Close-up of head.

155

This is a small snake, with a head slightly wider than the neck, a blunt snout, and a tail about 25% of the total length. Maximum size is less than 50 cm. The eye is relatively large, its diameter is equal to the length of the snout. The scales are smooth and arranged in 13 rows the entire length of the body. Ventrals 118–130 (males), 134–141 (females); subcaudals 63–75 (males), 58–69 (females); anal divided; upper labials 7, third and fourth border the eye. The head and body are dark brown, with two rows of small light spots on the back. The spots are conspicuous the entire length in young individuals, but fade near mid-body in older snakes. The white labial scales are edged with black. The underside is yellowish white, with or without fine dark dots. The outer edges of the ventrals have the same colour as the back.

The next species (*Liopeltis longicauda*) has similar scalation on the head and body, but is easily distinguished by its body stripes and neck chevron.

This species is one of the commonest snakes of the floor of lowland forests, from near sea level to about 600 m above sea level. Most records are of specimens seen by day under dead leaves or rocks. Probably it forages mainly at night over the leaf litter of the forest floor. The main prey is spiders.

Liopeltis longicauda
Striped Ground Snake

This species was originally described from Borneo, but has also been found in Java and Sumatra. It seems to be widespread in Sabah and Sarawak. Although it has not been reported from Kalimantan so far, it almost certainly occurs there. *Longi* = long, *cauda* = tail, referring to the relatively long tail.

A small snake, with a long slender tail about 35% of total length and its head wider than the neck. Maximum size is less than 50 cm. The eye is large, its diameter equalling the length of the snout. The scales are smooth and in 13 rows around the body. Ventrals 124 (males), 138 (female); subcaudals 92–105 (males); anal divided; upper labials usually 8, the third to fifth touching the eye. The head, neck, and first third or fourth of body are black, fading to dark reddish brown at mid-body, and then to black-brown at the rear. A white or yellow chevron splits the black of the neck and ends just behind the jaws. The body has five narrow light stripes, one down the centre of the back and two on each side; in adults the stripes end about mid-length. There is a tall, white triangle behind the eye. The belly is white; the outer ends of each ventral match the dark colour of the body.

In shape and size, this species closely resembles *L. baliodeirus*, but is easily recognized by the chevron on the nape and the light stripes. There is an additional, unnamed form of this genus in Borneo that differs from *L. longicauda* in lacking the chevron on the nape and the white marking behind the eye and from *L. baliodeirus* in lacking the rows of white dots along the back.

This is a species of lowland rain forests. Like the preceding species, it lives in the forest floor, hiding under dead leaves or rocks. Its food consists of spiders.

R.F. Inger

Liopeltis longicauda.

Liopeltis tricolor
Masked Ground Snake

This species was originally described from Java, but has been found in Peninsular Malaysia, Sumatra, and Borneo. The Bornean records are from Sarawak and Kalimantan. *Tri* = three, referring to the " three-coloured" body.

A small, slender snake with a relatively long tail (35% of total length) and slightly pointed snout. Maximum size less than 50 cm. The eye diameter is shorter than the snout length. The smooth scales form 15 rows in the forward half of the body, but reduce to 13 rows in the rear half. Ventral scales 153–160 (males), 159–171 (females); subcaudal scales 124–130 (males), 124–133 (females); anal divided; upper labials 7, fourth and fifth touching eye. The general colour is olive above and on sides, and yellowish or whitish below. A black streak beginning on the snout runs through the eye and fades out on the forepart of the body. There are no other markings on the upper part of the body. Low on the side a white stripe forms on adjacent edges of the first scale row and the ventrals and is bordered on the lower edge by a dark line running along the ventrals. There is no other pattern on the upper part of the body.

Very little is known about the natural history of this species. All of the observations of it in Borneo were made in lowland forests.

R.F. Inger

Liopeltis tricolor.

Pseudorabdion

This is a group of very small, shiny dark snakes. None is known to exceed 40 cm, all have short tails, all have 15 rows of smooth scales, all have small eyes, and all have some reduction of the usual complement of head shields. Some species have no loreal shield, others have no preocular, and one lacks both those head shields. These species secrete themselves under dead leaves, in the folds of tree buttresses, and under logs on the forest floor. In some forested areas they are very abundant. Probably all feed on earthworms. *Pseudo* = false, *rabdion* = stick, the name applied to some kind of Greek snake.

Pseudorabdion albonuchalis
Ring-Necked Litter Snake

Originally described from the Baram valley, Sarawak, this species has been discovered at several locations in Sarawak and Sabah. It has never been found outside of Borneo. *Albo* = white, *nuchalis* = nape, referring to the light ring around the neck.

A very small snake, with a short tail. The maximum known size is 39 cm. The tail forms 25% of the total length in males, but only 15% in females. The

R.F. Inger

Pseudorabdion albonuchalis.

159

head has a long loreal shield forming part of the border of the eye, but there is no preocular scale. The prefrontal shield touches the eye. Ventral scales 127–131 (males), 142–144 (females); subcaudals 58–64 (males), 41–46 (females); anal undivided; upper labials 5, with the third and fourth touching the eye. Black above, almost iridescent, slightly lighter below. The rear of the head and neck are encircled by a wide white ring that is interrupted on the throat.

Pseudorabdion albonuchalis.

R.B. Stuebing

160

This is a secretive snake, living under litter of the forest floor. It also burrows into the mat of hair roots common under leaf litter. It has never been found higher than 300 metres above sea level.

Pseudorabdion saravacensis is like *P. albonuchalis* in head scales, but has only a thin, narrowly interrupted yellow ring on the neck and a second thin ring a few scales behind the first one. It also has fewer ventral (109) and subcaudal (26) scales than *P. albonuchalis*.

Pseudorabdion collaris
Mocquard's Litter Snake

The species was first found in western Kalimantan, but is now known from a number of places in Sarawak and Sabah. It has not been found outside of Borneo. *Collaris* = a neck band, referring to the pattern of the type specimen.

A very small snake, with short tail and small eyes. Maximum known size is less than 25 cm, with the tail of females less than one eighth of the total. This species shows the most extreme reduction in head shields, lacking both loreal and preocular scales, so that the prefrontal touches two upper labials. Ventral scales 116–122 (males), 120–134 (females); subacudals 34–41 (males), 27–29 (females); anal undivided; upper labials 5, the third and fourth touching the eye. This species is shiny black with the belly slightly lighter. Only the type specimen (from Kalimantan) has a light band around the neck. It is possible that the ones we have seen represent a different species, but except for lacking a collar they match the type in all respects.

This is a species of the floor of lowland forests below 650 metres above sea level. Snakes have been found burrowed several cm in the soil, under dead leaves, and under rocks and logs. The diet consists of earthworms. One female contained three eggs.

Pseudorabdion longiceps
Lance-Headed Litter Snake

This species was described from Penang, Peninsular Malaysia, and has been found also in Sumatra, Sulawesi, and the Philippines. In Borneo it is known from Sarawak and Kalimantan. *Longi* = longer, *ceps* = head, referring to the slightly longer head of this species compared to others in the genus.

A very small snake, with a narrow head and short tail. Maximum known length is 25 cm. The tail makes up only one-tenth of the total in females, slightly more in males. There is no loreal shield. This is the only Bornean species of *Pseudorabdion* in which the prefrontal shield does not touch the eye. Ventral scales 129–134 (males), 136–147 (females); subcaudals 28–30 (males), 21–22 (females); anal not divided; upper labials 5, with the third and fourth touching the eye. The entire snake is dark brown or black with a thin yellow ring a few scales behind the head and usually a yellow spot on the side of the head behind the jaw. The yellow ring is absent in a small proportion of the population.

Like all the others in the genus, this species lives in and under the litter on forest floor. Although it is rather abundant in some areas, there is little information on its diet. One female contained two eggs.

Sibynophis geminatus
Striped Litter Snake

The type locality of this species is Java, but it has been reported from Sumatra through Java to Sarawak. We have found one in Sabah and it probably also occurs in Kalimantan. *Siby* = spear, *ophis* = snake; this probably refers to a fancied spear-like shape of its pattern. *Geminatus* = pair, probably referring to the pair of light stripes.

This is a small to medium-sized, slender snake, reaching a maximum length of just under one metre. The tail is moderately long, equaling more than one-third of the total. Its head is relatively narrow, and the eye rather large. All the body scales are smooth and arranged in 17 rows the full length of the body. Ventrals 144–180; subcaudals 73–96; upper labials eight, with the third to fifth touching the eye. This is a conspicuously striped snake. There is a dark brown to black stripe down the centre of the back, flanked on each side by a red or reddish brown stripe covering two and one-half scale rows. The top of the head is a rusty brown and the upper lip yellowish with narrow black borders on several of the labial scales. The underside is yellowish green in the first fourth of the body gradually changing into pale green. The outer ends of the ventrals have a black spot forming a narrow black stripe at the lower edge of the body.

THE BORNEO COMPANY

10 Locust Hill Road Cincinnati Ohio 45245

Tel/Fax: (513) 752-0848

E-mail: TheBorneoCompany@aol.com

PAID

For delivery to:

Mr. Justin McCann
54 Hewitt Avenue
Staten Island, NY 10301

Order Date:	01/17/01
Invoice Number:	01-03
Invoice Date:	01/21/01

Quantity	Description	Unit Price	Amount
1	*VOICES OF THE BORNEO RAINFOREST* (Recordings of rainforest birds and wildlife, identified to species, on compact disk.) Stuebing, R.B., 1995, 60 min. (1 CD, includes color illustrated interpretive booklet) Really Useful Co. Malaysia	10.00	10.00
	Subtotal		20.00

10 Feb 2001

Dear Justin,

   Thanks for your order, and especially
for the video. It really is a pleasure to see
again Danum Valley, and our nostalgia
level was raised almost to a painful level...
It is quite expertly done, + so congratulations
on your fine documentary. The
one clue for your fine documentary. The
portion on turtles was especially interesting
to me.

     With best regards,

The only two specimens of this snake recorded so far from Borneo were found in lowland forests below 400 metres of sea level. This species appears to be diurnal and is known in other parts of its geographic range to feed on skinks.

This species shows a lot of variation across its geographic range in colour of the stripes and in the number of ventral scales.

Sibynophis melanocephalus
White-Lipped Litter Snake

This species occurs from southern Thailand and Peninsular Malaysia to Borneo and Sumatra. In Borneo it has been found in many places in Sabah and Sarawak. *Sibyn* = spear, *ophis* = snake; *melano* = black, *cephalus* = head. The generic name presumably referred to the spear-like shape of head pattern in one species. The Bornean species has a dark head.

A small, relatively slender snake with a long tail. Maximum size is just over half a metre. Scales are smooth and in 17 rows throughout the body. Ventrals 167–177 (females), 170 (males); subcaudals 132–136; anal divided; upper labials 9, with 4th to 6th bordering eye. The eye is relatively large and its diameter is about equal to the length of the snout. This species is brown to reddish brown above, with the head a dark olive dotted with olive-yellow. The upper lip is white bordered above with a narrow black stripe. On each side of the midline of the back is of a row of short black crossbars on a lighter band forming an ill-defined light stripe. Low on each side is a row of small yellow spots. The underside is yellow with an orange tinge to the side near the end of the body. Each ventral scale has a round black spot near the side margin. The black-bordered white stripe on the lip and the long rows of small black bars are distinctive to this species.

A keelback, *Rhabdophis conspicillata*, usually has a dark bordered light streak on the lip, but it has keeled scales and rows of small light spots on the body.

The White-Lipped Litter Snake is most abundant at low elevations in rain forest, and a typical forest floor species. It has been found under logs, dead leaves and at the base of tree buttresses. Its main food seems to be forest floor skinks.

163

Stegonotus borneensis
Bornean Black Snake

The type locality is in central eastern Sarawak. The species was found there twice and several times in western Sabah. It has never been reported from outside Borneo. The generic name comes from *stegos* = roof, and *notos* = back, probably because of the ridged back in lowland specimens from Sarawak. This trait is not seen in Sabah specimens.

This is a medium-sized snake with a relatively short tail. Maximum known length is 1.3 m; the tail accounts for 22% of the total. The head is wider than the neck. The eye is small, its diameter being less than the distance between the eye and the nostril, and the pupil is vertically elliptical. The body scales are smooth and in 17 rows at mid-body. The anal scale is undivided. The ventrals have a weak, but distinct, keel near their outer ends. Ventrals 195 (male), 195–219 (females); caudals 77 (male), 79 (female); upper labials nine, with fourth and fifth touching the eye. All the upper surfaces, including the head, are very dark brown to black, without any

Stegonotus borneensis. Close-up of head.

Stegonotus borneensis.

markings. The ventral scales are light grey, each with a blackish band across the front edge.

Little is known of the habits of this species. It appears to be terrestrial and lives in forest from 200 to 1800 metres above sea level.

Zaocys carinatus
Keeled Rat Snake

This species was originally described from Borneo, but is known from most areas of South-east Asia, Sumatra, and into Palawan in the Philippines. It is not common in Borneo and we have never encountered one ourselves. The generic name is from *za* = very, and *okys* = swift, the name referring to the speed at which these snakes can move. *Carina* = keel or ridge, referring to the keeled scales on the back.

165

Except for the pythons and the king cobra, this is the largest snake in Asia, reaching a maximum length of four metres. Like its relative, *Zaocys fuscus*, it is proportionately rather slender and has a ridged back. The head is larger than the neck, but much narrower than most of the body. The snout is blunt and the eye large. There are 16–18 scale rows at mid-body and 12 just before the tail, all of them smooth except for the pair along the crest of the back, which are sharply keeled. Ventrals 208–215; subcaudals 110–118; anal divided; upper labials 8–10, usually the fifth and sixth touching the eye. Olive-brown, with or without black edgings to the scales. That pattern is particularly conspicuous on the tail and involves the subcaudals as well. Some individuals have indistinct yellow crossbars.

We know of only four reports of this species in Borneo. In Peninsular Malaysia it is a terrestrial species, although it probably is capable of climbing like its relative, *Zaocys fuscus*. It occurs both in native forests and tree plantations and is known to feed on rats.

Zaocys fuscus
White-Bellied Rat Snake

Originally described from Borneo, this rat snake is also known from Peninsular Malaysia and Sumatra. It occurs throughout Borneo. The species name is from *fuscus*, Latin, meaning dusky, referring to the coloration.

This is a large snake, reaching a length of three metres. For its size, this snake is relatively slender, has a ridged back, and has a long tail (about 36% of total length). The head is wider than the neck and the snout narrow, blunt, and about one and one-half times the diameter of the large eye. The scales are smooth and arranged in 16 rows at mid-body, reducing to 12 before the tail. Ventral scales 192–197 (males), 188–191 (females); subcaudals 155–161 (males), 161–165 (females); anal divided; upper labials usually 9, with the fifth and sixth bordering the eye. *Zaocys fuscus* has a generally brown coloration. The head is dark brown above and white below. The body is very dark, almost black on the neck and fore parts, becoming more brown gradually. The two lowest scale rows and the outer parts of the ventrals remain dark, forming a dark stripe in the rear half of the body and a sharply defined black stripe low on the side of the tail. Usually, the outer tip of each ventral scale has a white spot, giving the dark stripe a dotted appearance. The entire underside is white.

(Above). *Zaocys fuscus* and (below). Close-up of head.

Zaocys fuscus is relatively common in lowland rain forests. It is a versatile species, being at home on the ground, in water, and up in vegetation. We have seen individuals swimming in large rivers as well as up in trees as high as six metres above ground. It probably feeds on birds and mammals. Despite its size, and though it looks fearsome, this is not an aggressive snake. Its bite is harmless.

Natricinae

This group is known as "water snakes" in much of the Temperate Zone, but many of its members in Borneo have rather terrestrial habits, though often found in the general vicinity of streams. Several species have the last pair of posterior maxillary (= upper jaw) teeth much enlarged, and grooved. These species may also be venomous, but the effects of this venom on humans is not well documented. Because of their tendency to bite, however, natricines should be treated with caution.

Amphiesma flavifrons
White-Nosed Water Snake

Originally described from the slopes of Mount Kinabalu, Sabah, this species has been found throughout Sabah and Sarawak. It probably also is widespread in Kalimantan. *Amphi* = dual, *esma* of unknown meaning. *Flavi* = yellow, *frons* = forehead, referring to the light spot on the top of the snout.

A medium-sized water snake reaching a maximum of around 75 cm. The tail is moderately long, slightly less than one-third of total length. The keeled scales are in 19 rows until just past the middle of the body at which point the number is reduced to 17. Ventral scales 149–154 (males), 148–157 (females); subcaudals 100–101 (males), 92–94 (females); anal divided; upper labials 7 or 8, with the fourth and fifth touching the eye. The general colour is dark greenish black, but the most distinctive feature is a large yellowish white (adults) or bright white (juveniles) spot on the snout. Juveniles have paired white spots down the centre of the back and along the sides. In some adults these light spots have become darkened. The belly is white, with alternating black spots covering about one-third of each ventral.

R.B. Stuebing

Amphiesma flavifrons.

This is one of the two most common snakes seen along clear, small streams in primary or secondary forests inland. (The other is the Rufous-Sided Water Snake.) It is immediately recognizable because of its habit of swimming with its head out of water, showing its prominent white snout. It is active both by day and at night. It feeds on a variety of frogs, tadpoles, and frog eggs. Although most common at low elevations, it has been found as high as 1375 metres on Mount Kinabalu.

169

Amphiesma frenata
Bridled Water Snake

This species was found originally on the slope of Mount Murud, Sarawak, at 610 metres above sea level. So far it is known only from several localities in Sarawak. *Frenatus* = bridle or rein, referring to the white chevron on the neck, which resembles the bridle of a horse.

A small water snake, with a long tail and a large eye. The tail is about one-third the total length and the diameter of the eye is more than twice the depth of the upper lip. Maximum known size is 61 cm. All the scales are keeled. There are 17 scale rows in the front half of the body and 15 thereafter. Ventral scales 164–166; subcaudals 112–116; upper labials 8, with third to fifth touching the eye. The general ground colour is brown, with pairs of black bars on each side. Each pair of black bars encloses a light bar that is cream in the fore part of the body, but becomes progressively darker in the rear of the body. The most conspicuous pattern element is a slender white chevron on the neck, with arms running down and forward to cover all the upper labial scales. A short black stripe covering the lower parts of the last three labial scales separates the white chevron from the lip. The first three upper labials have a small black spot. The top of the head is dark with small black spots. The belly is grey with large brown and black spots.

Almost nothing is known of this rare snake. Both recorded specimens were found in rain forest. One was discovered under a log.

The narrow white chevron resembles the pattern in *Rhabdophis chrysarga*, but that species does not have a black stripe on the edges of the last upper labials and has less than 90 subcaudals.

Amphiesma sarawacensis
Checker-Bellied Water Snake

This species was originally described on the basis of specimens from Matang, Sarawak. It appears to be common in all parts of Borneo and has been found in the highlands of Peninsular Malaysia. *Sarawacensis* = referring to the site of its original discovery.

A small to medium-sized snake with a moderate tail accounting for about 30% of the total length. Maximum size is about 75 cm. All the body scales are keeled and are arranged in 17 rows throughout most of the body. Ventral scales 134–145 (males), 136–146 (females); subcaudals 75–86 (males), 81–84 (females); upper labials 8, the third to fifth touching the eye. This is a dark olive to brown snake. The centre of the back has a row of black squares or rectangles. A row of small light yellowish squares runs along the side and below that is another row of small black squares. The pattern becomes obscured in older snakes. The head is dark olive brown or black, with a yellow or white upper lip. Each of the upper labial scales is edged with black. The belly is most distinctive. It has a bold checkered pattern of black and white. In some snakes the black dominates, especially towards the rear of the body.

This species occurs only in forests, mainly at low elevations but is reasonably common on the slopes of Mount Kinabalu as high as 1675 metres above sea level. In Peninsular Malaysia it has been seen only in the highlands. It wanders farther from streams than most members of its group, but shares their diet of frogs and toads and even takes frog eggs. Like all the Bornean water snakes, this species lays eggs. Clutch size is small, four to five.

Hydrablabes periops
Dwarf Water Snake

This species was described from a specimen collected at Matang, not far from Kuching, Sarawak. It has since been found at other places in Sarawak and in Sabah. It probably occurs over much of Borneo. It is not known from any other land mass. The generic name comes from *hydro* = water, and *ablabes* = harmless; reference is to the habitat and harmless nature of the snake. *Peri* = around, *ops* = eye, referring to the ring of small scales encircling the eye.

A small snake of medium girth, rarely exceeding half a metre in length. The tail is rather short, about one-fifth of the total length. The head is small, scarcely wider than the neck, and narrower than the body. The eye is small and has a round pupil. The distinctive thing about the head is that the eye is separated from the upper labials by a ring of small scales. The body scales are smooth and arranged in 15 or 17 rows at mid-length. Ventral scales 189–209 (males), 179–193 (females); subcaudals 62–76 (males), 56–69 (females); upper labials 8 or 9. *Hydrablabes periops* is dark brown, usually without much pattern. Some individuals have a light brown stripe on the side; the stripe is most evident in the front half of the body and may have narrow

R.B. Stuebing

Hydrablabes periops.

black borders. The rest of the body usually has small, obscure dark spots. The ventrals are yellowish or grey with brown outer ends and may have narrow dark margins.

Hydrablabes periops seems to be fully aquatic. All those we have seen were swimming in small creeks in primary forest between 150 and 600 metres above sea level.

A second species of this genus, *Hydrablabes praefrontalis* (Mocquard) described from "Kinabalu" actually may not be a separate species. It has the same ring of small scales around the eye, smooth scales in 17 rows, and the generally olive or dark brown coloration of *H. periops*. The principal difference between the two is that in *H. praefrontalis* the prefrontal scales on the top of the head are fused into one.

Macropisthodon flaviceps
Orange-Lipped Water Snake

This species was described from Borneo, but has been found in southern Thailand, Peninsular Malaysia, and Sumatra. In Borneo, it has been recorded from Sarawak and western Kalimantan. The generic name is taken from

172

makros = large, *opistho* = behind, and *don* = tooth, referring to the enlarged tooth at the rear of the upper jaw. *Flavus* = yellow, and *ceps* = head, referring to the colour of the head.

This medium-sized, heavy-bodied snake, rarely exceeds one metre in length and has a short tail. The head is wider than the front part of the body. The rear tooth of the upper jaw is conspicuously larger and longer than the other teeth. All the body scales are strongly keeled except for the first (lowest) row. There are 19 scale rows at mid-body, reducing to 15 before the tail. Ventral scales 124–133 (males), 128–135 (females); subcaudals 53–60 (males), 47–57 (females); upper labials 8, with the fourth and fifth touching the eye. Adults have a brown or yellowish head, with a rusty orange upper lip and a whitish chin. The neck is olive-brown with a wide black collar. The remainder of the body is dark brown or black, with narrow white or light yellow crossbands that become indistinct towards the tail. Juveniles are brownish and more conspicuously banded.

This species lives in coastal swamps, sluggish streams, and even in roadside ditches. It appears to be abundant in Sarawak, though not often

R.B. Stuebing

Macropisthodon flaviceps.

173

seen. The principal prey are frogs and we have records of them eating large toads, despite the poisonous skin of the prey.

This is an irascible snake, like many water snakes, and should be handled with caution. Its enlarged rear tooth can inflict a painful wound, and there is the possibility that its saliva may be venomous. In Peninsular Malaysia it has been observed raising the head and flattening the neck when threatened.

Macropisthodon flaviceps.

174

Macropisthodon rhodomelas
Blue-Necked Water Snake

The original specimen was found in Java, but the species is known from southern Thailand, Peninsular Malaysia, Sumatra, Java, and Borneo. It has been found at a number of places in Sabah and Sarawak, and probably occurs throughout the island. *Rhodon* = rose or red, and *melas* = black. The reference is to the combination of colours on young snakes.

This is a medium-sized snake, rarely reaching more than 75 cm. The tail is relatively short, accounting for 17–21% of the total length. The head is wider than the neck, with a wide, rounded snout. All the scales are keeled except for those in the first (lowest) row, which are also the largest. There are 19 scale rows until near the tail. Ventral scales 133–139 (males), 132–144 (females); subcaudals 52–64 (males), 50–64 (females); upper labials 8, the fourth and fifth touching the eye. The general colour of head and body is rusty brown, reddish in juveniles. The neck has a wide black chevron open

Macropisthodon rhodomelas.

175

forwards and drawn out in the rear to a thin black stripe that runs on the crest of the back the length of the body. The side of the neck below the black chevron is powder blue and the sides behind the chevron are reddish. The brown body has a series of thin black lines extending downward and forward from the black vertebral stripe, which is usually bordered by small white spots. The ventrals are pink with rusty coloured ends, the two colours separated by a series of small black spots.

Macropisthodon rhodomelas lives on the ground in primary and secondary forests at low elevations. At some places it seems to be very abundant. The main prey consists of frogs. It lays at least 25 eggs. We have not found this species to be aggressive, but because of the long rear tooth it should be handled with great care.

Opisthotropis typica
Corrugated Water Snake

The first specimen collected came from "Kinabalu," without further specification as to elevation. So far as we know, this species has been collected three more times—in the lowlands of the east coast of Sabah and eastern and south-western Sarawak. *Opistho* = rear or back; *tropis* = keel or ridge, the generic name presumably referring to the strongly keeled back = *typica*, probably because the original describer, Mocquard, intended this species to be the type of a new genus, which was later combined with an existing one.

A slender snake, with a flattened head and rounded snout. The eye is small, its diameter less than half the length of the snout and shorter than the distance between the eye and the lip. The maximum known size is 50 cm, the tail making up 25% of the total. The head scales are unusual for a member of the family Colubridae. All Bornean colubrids except this one have the upper lip set with a single row of scales (the upper labials) bordering the mouth. In *Ophisthotropis* , some of the upper labials are divided horizontally into large upper and small lower portions. Also in the great majority of colubrids the eye meets two or three of the upper labials; in this species the eye is surrounded by a ring of small scales separating it from the labials. The scales are rough, each having a central ridge or keel on which are set small knobs. In addition, the body scales and those on top of the head have fine lines or

R.B. Stuebing

R.B. Stuebing

(Above). *Opisthotropis typica* and (below). Close-up of head.

striations. There are 21 scale rows behind the head, 19 at mid-body, and 17 just before the vent. Ventrals 146–176; subcaudals 82–96. Upper labials 11. General colour olive or purple brown in preservative; probably dark brown in life. The undersides of the head and body are pale whitish or a dirty yellow. The snake is completely without any markings.

This species seems to be an aquatic or riparian snake. Two specimens were found at the edge of small forest streams and one in the water of a forest swamp. Nothing is known about the diet.

Oreocalamus hanitschi
Mountain Reed Snake

Found originally on Mount Kinabalu in northern Sabah, it has also been found in the highlands in southwestern Sabah and on the Kelabit plateau in northern Sarawak. One specimen was collected on Mount Brinchang in the Cameron Highlands of Peninsular Malaysia. *Oreo* = mountain, *calamus* = reed, referring to the montane habitat of a snake superficially like *Calamaria*; *Hanitsch* = name of the collector, formerly head of the Raffles Museum, now the National Museum of Singapore.

A short, thick-bodied snake with a short, sharply pointed tail. Maximum known size is 57 cm and the tail is about one-eighth of the total. The head is the same width as the neck at the rear and tapers towards the narrow snout. The scales are smooth and in 17 rows the full length of the body. Ventral scales 129–132 (males), 125–127 (females); subcaudals 26–32 (males), 21–23 (females); upper labials 7, with the fourth and fifth bordering the eye. Light tan above with darker brown scales scattered to form a zigzag pattern on the back. Low on the side dark scales form an almost continuous stripe. The lips are barred black and white. A thin dark streak passes through the eye and may continue for a short distance along the body. The rear of the head and neck usually have a dark, wide, V-shaped mark pointing forwards. The belly is pale tan with faint dark dots down the centre and dark spots at the outer edges of the ventrals forming a dark stripe. The tail has three dark stripes.

This species lives on the floor of montane oak forests, hiding under debris and rocks. It feeds on earthworms. Bornean records for this species lie between 1120 and 1525 metres above sea level. The single record from Peninsular Malaysia is from 1700 metres.

178

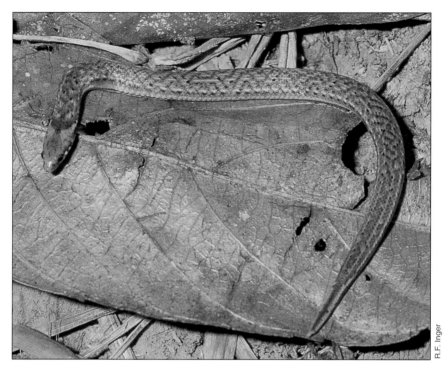

R.F. Inger

Oreocalamus hanitschi.

Pseudoxenodon baramensis
Baram Water Snake

This species, originally described from Mount Dulit at 1000 metres, has been found only a few times since and in every case from upland areas of Sarawak. *Pseudo* = false, *xeno* = strange, *don* = tooth; implying this genus is not the same as the genus *Xenodon*; *baramensis* = referring to the Baram drainage in which the origin specimen was caught.

A medium-sized, heavy-bodied snake, with a short tail. Maximum known size is 70 cm. The tail accounts for less than one-fifth of the total length. The scales are weakly keeled; usually only the middle three rows are keeled in the front third of the body, with all rows except the outer becoming keeled towards the rear of the body. On the neck, the scales have an odd overlapping pattern suggesting that this snake can spread its neck when agitated. There are 19 rows of scales in the first half of the body, the number

179

dropping to 15 just a few centimeters beyond that point. Ventral scales 132–134; subcaudals 45–47; upper labials 8, with fourth and fifth touching eye. The body has a dark chain-like pattern. Just behind the head is a large, thin, black V-shaped mark pointing forwards and with the arms running backward and downward along the sides. The belly is yellowish, dusted with brown at the front and becoming increasingly darker towards the rear.

This is one of the least known species in Borneo. Nothing is known about its behaviour or favoured environment.

Rhabdophis chrysarga
Speckle-Bellied Keelback

This species was originally described from Java, but has since been found all over South-east Asia. It is known from all parts of Borneo. *Rhabdo* = striped, *ophis* = snake, referring to the striped pattern in some species of the genus; *chryso* = golden, *argus* = bright, referring to the bright rusty golden colour of the front part of the body in juveniles.

A moderate-sized species, with a relatively short tail. Maximum size is about 75 cm. The tail forms about one-fourth of the total length. The scales are strongly keeled except for the first row and there are 19 rows in the first half of the body and 17 thereafter. Ventral scales 145–152 (males), 139–153 (females); subcaudals 74–87 (males), 67–77 (females); upper labials 9, with

R.B. Stuebing

Rhabdophis chrysarga. Close-up of head.

180

R.B. Stuebing

Rhabdophis chrysarga.

the fourth to sixth touching the eye. Juveniles are more brightly coloured than adults. The top of the head in young snakes is dark greyish green with a reddish tint near the snout. The upper labials below the eye are white with narrow dark edges. There is a jet black band on the neck about the length of the head, split by a narrow white chevron. Behind the black band is a rusty or golden orange area of varying length. The centre of the back has a row of alternating yellow and brown oblongs, bordered below by rows of black and smaller yellow squares. In adults, the white chevron and black band are clear, but the yellow areas are not as bright and tend towards olive at the rear of the body. The ventral scales are yellowish mottled with brown. Towards the rear of the body brown spots tend to form a pair of dark stripes, especially under the tail.

181

Rhabdophis chrysarga is a common snake of forested lowland areas, but also rather abundant on the slopes of Mount Kinabalu up to about 1000 metres. This species is often seen on forest floor at some distance from stream banks. The main food is frogs. *Rhabdophis chrysarga* lays from three to ten eggs. These snakes should be handled with caution as they frequently attempt to bite.

A similar species, *Rhabdophis conspicillata,* has a narrow white half-ring on a dark neck, but the ring is clearly incomplete.

Rhabdophis conspicillata
Red-Bellied Keelback

This species was originally described from Matang, near Kuching, Sarawak. It is widely distributed in lowland forests in Borneo and has also been found in Peninsular Malaysia. *Conspicillatus* = spectacle, but the significance in this case is unclear.

A small water snake with a short tail. Maximum known size is slightly more than half a metre. The tail is about one-fifth of total length. The keeled scales are arranged in 19 rows in the front two-thirds, and in 17 rows after

Rhabdophis conspicillata. Close-up of head.

182

Rhabdophis conspicillata. Close-up of head.

that. Ventral scales 145–149 (males), 141–152 (females); subcaudals 51–52 (males), 52–60 (females); upper labials 8, with the third to fifth touching the eye. The general pattern is checkered black and brown. The pattern is more conspicuous in juvenile snakes. The side of the head is striped; the edge of the upper lip has a narrow brown stripe followed above by a wider white stripe and above that a brown stripe beginning at the lower rear corner of the eye and above that a white stripe that runs back through the neck. The nape and neck have two narrow, interrupted, white rings that meet the upper white stripe from the eye. The ventrals are yellowish with a dark rear edge to each and many fine brown dots or specklings over the rest.

This species, like *Amphiesma sarawacensis*, wanders far from water. Most of those we have seen were moving across the forest floor at night or resting under dead leaves or in the folds of tree buttresses by day. There is no information on diets, but we presume that the species feeds heavily on frogs like other members of the group. *Rhabdophis conspicillata* is very abundant in some areas and rare in others.

Rhabdophis murudensis
Fire-Lipped Keelback

This species was originally described from Mount Murud, in eastern Sarawak, and is endemic to Borneo. It has only been found at the type locality, and on Mount Kinabalu. *Murudensis* refers to Mount Murud, the type locality.

A small to medium-sized water snake reaching up to about one metre in length. The tail is about 20% of total length. The scales are all strongly keeled except for the outer row, which is smooth, and the second row, which is faintly keeled. The scales are arranged in 19 rows in the front third of the body, and in 17 rows after that. Ventral scales 180 (males), 180–185

Rhabdophis murudensis.

184

(females); subcaudals 97 (males), 72–80 (females); anal divided; upper labials 9, with the fourth to sixth touching the eye. There is a deep groove down the midline of the rear head shields, containing venom glands about which little is known in this species. The head and nape are brown, and upper lip bright vermillion (reddish-orange). The eye is brown with light green segment in the dorsal portion. A portion of the neck is bright reddish-orange with regularly arranged black spots. The body is grey with short, indistinct black crossbars. A row of light spots associated with the ends of these dark markings appears at mid body and runs down the back, converging to a single row anterior to the vent and extending to the end of the tail.

This snake has been found only between 1000–1700 m above sea level, so that it appears to be strictly submontane. A few specimens were collected in 1929, and none were found again until the late 1970s, when the species began to be seen after a new road was constructed within the Kinabalu Park Headquarters area. Tan Fui Lian kept a specimen alive on a diet of frogs for some years in the laboratory at the Park.

As in some other natricines, the rearmost teeth of *Rhabdophis murudensis* are greatly enlarged, and it is likely, judging from the bright colours of this snake, that it is venomous. (In Hong Kong, there was a fatality from the bite of a related natricine species, *Rhabdophis subminiata*). This snake should be treated with great caution, and not handled.

Xenochrophis maculata
Large-Eyed Water Snake

This species was first found in south-eastern Kalimantan and has since been seen at many places in Sarawak and in western Sabah. It also occurs in Peninsular Malaysia and Sumatra. *Xeno* = stranger or strange, *ochro* = pale yellow, *ophis* = snake; the generic name probably refers to characteristics of the first species described in this genus. *Maculata* = spotted, referring to the rows of small black squares on the back.

This is a medium-sized snake, with a relatively long tail (about one-third the total length) and a large eye. The diameter of the eye is almost twice the depth of the upper lip. Maximum size is about one metre. All the body scales are keeled and arranged in 19 rows in the front three-fifths of the body, dropping to 17 rows after that. Ventrals 138–150 (males), 144–151 (females); subcaudals 108–114 (males), 103–116 (females); upper labials 8 or 9, usually

Bjorn Lardner

Xenochrophis maculata.

the fourth to the sixth border the eye. The general coloration is dark. The centre of the back is dark brown or grey with a pair of rows of small black squares. This dark band is bordered by an indistinct, narrow, lighter brown strip and that in turn by another darker band. There is usually another row of small black squares in this outer dark band. The head is dark brown or black, except for the white or yellowish upper lip. Each of the upper labial scales is edged with black. The belly is yellow, with each ventral scale having a black spot at its outer ends.

This species lives along the banks of small streams in lowland rain forest. It feeds exclusively on frogs and toads.

The rare species *Amphiesma petersi* is very similar to the Large-Eyed Water Snake in general coloration and size, but it differs in having a much smaller eye (diameter less than twice its distance from the lip) and fewer than 95 subcaudals.

Xenochrophis trianguligera
Red-Sided or Triangle Keelback

Originally described from Java, this species has been found over much of Peninsular Malaysia, Sumatra, and all parts of Borneo. *Trianguli* = triangles, *gera* = to bear, referring to the conspicuous red or orange triangles on the side of the neck and fore part of the body.

A medium to large water snake, with maximum size just over one metre. The eye is not as large as in the Large-Eyed Water Snake. The tail is about one-fourth the total length. The keeled scales are in 19 rows in the front half

Xenochrophis trianguligera.

R.B. Stuebing

of the body and reduced to 17 rows beyond that. Ventral scales 134–142 (males), 135–145 (females); subcaudals 86–97 (males), 86–92 (females); upper labial scales usually 9, with the fourth to sixth touching the eye. This is a blackish snake with conspicuous reddish or orange-red triangles on the side of the neck and front third or so of the body. The red areas become progressively darker, especially in older snakes, turning into olive-brown or grey. The black areas between the red triangles are also triangular in shape and persist to the end of the body. At the front part of the body the black areas have reddish centres. The centre of the back has a row of oblong black markings. The head is dark with a white lip; several of the upper labial scales have narrow black edges. The black triangles of the sides send narrow fingers of black across the belly, which is whitish otherwise.

Although stream banks are the usual habitat of this very common snake, it also occurs around small ponds and in swamps. At all these sites, it preys on frogs, tadpoles, and frog eggs. Five to eight eggs are laid. It is not limited to primary forest, and is often seen at the edges of wet fields and even in villages. It is most abundant at lower elevations but has been found as high as 1350 metres above sea level.

Elapidae
Cobras, Kraits, Coral and Sea Snakes

The Elapidae include the terrestrial Elapinae, or cobras, kraits and coral snakes, and two subfamilies of sea snakes, the Laticaudinae and the Hydrophiinae. They have distinctively broad, in some cases rather blunt snouts, with no loreal scale. Most terrestrial elapids also have unpaired subcaudals. All have permanently erect, short fangs at the front of the maxillary (upper jaw) bone, and are dangerously venomous.

Elapinae

Bungarus fasciatus
Banded Krait

Originally described from Bengal, eastern India, this species has been found throughout South-east Asia. In Borneo, it is known from coastal areas of Sarawak, Kalimantan and Sabah. There is one record from the interior of Sabah. *Bungarus* is simply a "New Latin" name for this genus; *fascia* = a band, referring to the colour pattern.

A medium-sized snake, reaching about 1.5 m with a tail about 8–11% of total length. The head is blunt and not wider than the neck. The back bone, covered with a row of enlarged scales, forms a conspicuous ridge down the back. The tail is blunt or club-shaped as if severed in an accident. All the scales under the tail, the subcaudals, are undivided. Like all members of the cobra family, the species lacks a loreal scale. The body scales are in 15 rows. Ventral scales 213–234 (males), 217–230 (females); subcaudals undivided, 28–37 (males), 32–34 (females); anal undivided; upper labials 7, with the third and fourth touching the eye. This is a conspicuously banded black and white or black and yellow snake. The top of the head has a black V-shaped marking that widens to form the first black band on the body. The sides of the head are dusky whitish to yellowish. The black bands do not encircle the snake in the first third of the body. The light spaces between the bands become increasingly dusky past mid-body.

The Banded Krait is mainly a coastal snake, often found in or near peat swamp forests or forest remnants, including estates. It also occurs around houses in some parts of its range. It is terrestrial and feeds mainly on snakes and other small vertebrates. Like all kraits, this species is relatively non-aggressive. If only mildly threatened, it usually tries to hide the head under coils of the body. However, the bite is very serious and can be fatal. The tombstone in Kota Kinabalu of an estate manager bitten by a banded krait is testimony to this fact. (See p. 35)

Baby cobras (*Naja sumatrana*) are also banded black and white, but their dark bands always encircle the body and the head is a uniform light brown. Sea snakes and even file snakes are banded, but are never found in mainland, fresh-water swamps.

Bungarus fasciatus. (Close-up of head)

190

Bungarus fasciatus.

R.B. Stuebing

Bungarus flaviceps
Yellow-Headed Krait

This species, originally described from Java, is distributed from Burma and southern Indochina, through Peninsular Malaysia, Sumatra, and Java. It has been found in most parts of Borneo. *Flavi* = yellow, *ceps* = head, referring to the head colour, which is golden-yellow in some populations. A subspecies, *Bungarus flaviceps baluensis* is reasonably common on Mount Kinabalu and Mount Trus Madi at around 200–750 m above sea level.

191

This is a large snake, reaching a length of two metres. The tail is short, equaling less than 15% of the total length and ending in a blunt, though narrow, tip. The subcaudal scales at the base of the tail are single and the rest are paired, although in some individuals only those near the end of the tail are paired. The backbone forms a conspicuous ridge down the centre of the back. The head is blunt and about the same width as the neck. The eye is moderate in size and is slightly larger than its distance from the mouth. The smooth scales of the body are in 13 rows, with the vertebral scale row much larger than adjacent scales. Ventral scales 219–225 (males), 206–218 (females); subcaudals single up to about half the length of the tail, then divided, 47–52 (males), 42–50 (females); anal undivided, upper labials 6 or 7, third and fourth touching the eye.

Basically, this is a black snake with a yellow or red head and tail. Populations in Peninsular Malaysia have red head and tail, whereas those parts in many snakes from Borneo are yellowish-brown to bright yellow.

R.B. Stuebing

Bungarus flaviceps.

Most of the body behind the neck is glossy blue-black, often with a thin straw-coloured or whitish line down the back. Most of the variation in colour involves the rear of the snake. The red on the tail may extend forward one-fourth to one-half of the body length. In some snakes, the red area is without markings. In others, the red area is crossed by narrow black bands completely encircling the body in sets of three; within each of these sets, the black bands are separated by narrow white bands. The sets of black bands are separated by much wider red areas. The number of sets of black bands varies from zero to seven. The ground colour of the belly in all those we have seen is pink to yellowish, with a heavy dusting of black in the fore part of the body and black rings near the rear in those snakes with black banding.

The Yellow-Headed Krait is a forest species, living in primary and old secondary forests from near sea level to about 750 m. Little is known of its diet, but it probably feeds on snakes and other small vertebrates. Like the Banded Krait, this species is not aggressive. It initially hides it head under leaf litter when disturbed, but if handled roughly will attempt to bite. It must be treated as a very dangerous species.

The Blue Coral Snake has a blue-black body and red head and tail, but it has a thin bluish white stripe on each side of the back and a wider white stripe low on the side.

Maticora bivirgata
Blue Coral Snake

Described from Java, this species is known from southern Thailand to Borneo. It occurs throughout the island, below about 700 metres. The origin of the generic name *Maticora* is unclear; the species name is from *bi* = two, and *virgata* = branches, either referring to the pair of light stripes on the sides, or perhaps to the pattern of specimens from Java, which have a conspicuous light Y-shaped mark on the top rear of the head.

This is a slender, medium-sized snake, reaching a maximum length of just under two metres. The tail is short, about 10% of total length, and ends in a sharp point. The head is rather small and not wider than the neck. The scales are smooth and in 13 rows the full length of the body. Ventral scales 243–304; subcaudals 37–49; upper labials 6, with the third and fourth touching the eye. The back and sides are blue-black, with a pair of sky-blue stripes on each side. The upper stripe is really just a thin line, and the lower,

R.F. Inger

Maticora bivirgata.

wider one is about one-half scale wide. The head, belly, and entire tail are coral red. In some individuals, the upper surface of the tail has three or four widely spaced, diamond-shaped, black spots.

Maticora bivirgata lives in both primary and secondary forests in well-drained areas of the lowlands, up to about 600 m. Although its coloration is conspicuous, this species is rather secretive. It is most often seen moving across dead leaves on the forest floor. The diet consists largely of other snakes, and Tweedie reports a case of a *M. bivirgata* that had eaten another coral snake, *M. intestinalis*.

One of the remarkable features of the coral snakes of the genus *Maticora* is that they have extraordinarily long venom glands. Instead of being confined to the head, as in all other venomous snakes of South-east Asia, the glands of *Maticora* extend almost one-third of the length of the body. Despite this impressive weapon, *Maticora bivirgata* is a docile, non-aggressive snake. In fact, if threatened, it usually tries to hide its head under leaves or under a coil of the body and curl the bright red tail up in the air to form a cork-screw spiral. However docile this species, it should be treated as very dangerous.

The related Bornean species, *Maticora intestinalis*, has wider, reddish or brown stripes on the back and black bands across the belly. The Red-Headed Krait, *Bungarus flaviceps*, either lacks stripes on the back or has a thin light-coloured line on the back; also the rear part of the body in front of the tail is usually red and banded with black.

Maticora intestinalis
Banded Coral Snake

The exact place of origin for the type specimen is unknown, but the species occurs from southern Thailand to Java and Sulawesi. It has been found throughout Borneo. *Intestinum* = intestine or intestinal; this may refer to the long, thin shape of the snake.

This is a small, slender species, rarely exceeding half metre in length. The head is small, not wider than the neck, and the tail is only about 6–8% of the total length. All the body scales are smooth and in 13 rows the full

Maticora intestinalis. Close-up of head.

195

length of the body. Ventral scales 206–233 (males), 222–240 (females); subcaudals 21–26 (males), 21–24 (females); anal undivided; upper labials 6, with the third and fourth touching the eye. The coloration is variable, but basically this is a brown or blackish snake with stripes. A light brown or tan stripe high on the side appears in all individuals. Some individuals have a scarlet stripe down the centre of the back, separated from the brown stripe by a narrow blackish stripe. In some specimens, the scarlet stripe runs only a short distance behind the head; in others it is completely absent. A thin white or light blue stripe runs between the outer end of the ventrals and the lowest scale row. The head is medium brown, but reddish in juvenile snakes. The underside is yellow, white, or coral red, with a series of black cross bands, each two or three ventrals wide. The underside of the tail is red with black cross bands. Rarely, snakes lack the black cross bands.

Maticora intestinalis lives in primary and secondary forests below 750 m above sea level. It has also been found in gardens or compounds in cities (Kuching). It is a secretive species, usually resting under dead leaves or logs and sometimes just below the surface of the soil. It feeds mainly on small snakes, for example, species of *Calamaria* and *Liopeltis* that use the same kind of resting places.

The Banded Coral Snakes have a distinct defensive display. When disturbed, they flatten the body and raise the tail to show the bright red underside. Occasionally, a snake may flip over exposing the bright pattern of the belly. Although these snakes are not aggressive and have very small

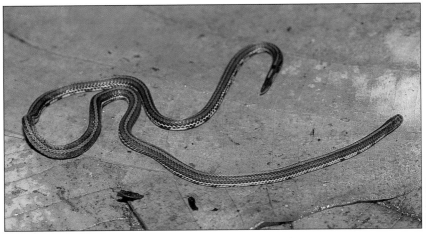

Maticora intestinalis.

196

Maticora intestinalis in its defensive posture.

mouths, they should be left alone, for a bite may have very serious consequences. Its long thin shape has inspired the local (Malay) name of *ular tali kasut*, or "shoelace snake", and it is regarded as dangerous. The Ibans of Sarawak refer to this species as *ular tedung babi* ("pig cobra"). According to the story behind the name, bearded (forest) pigs rooting in the leaf litter of the forest, if bitten on the snout by this coral snake will drop dead within minutes.

Naja sumatrana
Sumatran Cobra

The type locality for this cobra is Sumatra, but it also occurs in extreme southern Thailand and Peninsular Malaysia. It is widespread in Borneo at low elevations and occasionally higher up in disturbed areas. The generic name is based on the Indian name for cobra. The specific name refers to the type locality.

This cobra is a medium-sized snake, rarely more than 1.5 m in length, with a short tail about one-seventh of the total. The head is wider than the neck and the snout is short. The eye is rather large, its diameter being about equal to the distance to the nostril. The third upper labial scale is large and

R.B. Stuebing

Indraneil Das

(Above and below). *Naja sumatrana*.

touches both the eye and the nasal scale. Unlike the King Cobra, this species has no enlarged scales behind the parietals on top of the head. The smooth scales are in 21–25 rows on the neck (allowing for the hood), decreasing to 15–17 at mid-body. Ventrals 187–191 (males), 191–206 (females); subcaudals (first six or so undivided) 49–53 (males), 42–47 (females); upper labial scales seven, the third and fourth touching the eye. Adults are almost completely black, although the head is usually dark olive. The lip and throat are yellowish. Juveniles (less than 40 cm) are black with a white chevron at the rear of the hood and narrow white rings on the rest of the body. The white rings are gradually invaded by black, and by the time a young cobra reaches 45–50 cm it is completely black like the adults.

Although primarily a forest species, the Sumatran Cobra also thrives in secondary growth and even enters gardens, parks and house compounds in urban areas. Its diet consists mainly of rodents. It is not an aggressive snake, but of course it must be treated as very dangerous. Adults of the Common Racer, which is dark above and on the sides, are often mistaken for a cobra, but the white belly of the racer is quite distinctive.

Ophiophagus hannah
King Cobra

The type locality for this species (first described in 1836) is unknown, but the King Cobra is widely distributed throughout South-east Asia. It occurs in Borneo at elevations below 1000 metres. *Ophio* = snake, *phagus* = "to eat", referring to the principal diet of the species, which is other snakes. The meaning of *hannah* is unclear.

King cobras reach an impressive maximum length of almost 6 metres, though individuals greater than four metres long are uncommon in Borneo. The head is broad behind the eyes, while the snout is rather short. The eye is large, and its distance to the nostril is about one and a half times its diameter. The pupil is round. The parietal scales on the top of the head are usually followed by small neck scales in most snakes, but in the King Cobra the parietals are followed by another pair of very large scales. There are 15 smooth rows of scales. Ventrals 240–252 (males), 254–259 (females); subcaudals (unpaired in the initial half of the tail) 113–117 (males), 99–104 (females); anal undivided; upper labials 7, the third one enlarged and bordering both the nasal scale (nostril) and eye. The head is tan or light brown contrasting with the darker upper body, which ranges from a dark olive green to dark brown. The chin and throat are creamy white, becoming grey just beyond the underside of the neck, and progressively darker grey towards the anus. Juvenile king cobras look strikingly different from the adults. The head is black, with a yellow tip on the snout and two broken yellow bands across the top of the head, one in front and the other behind the eyes. The nape has an inverted V-shaped band. The body is glossy black with regularly spaced bright yellow rings, narrowest and chevron-shaped over the middle of the back. The underside is light yellow.

The King Cobra is primarily a forest species, though occasionally encountered at forest edge or in regenerating habitats such as old shifting cultivation or plantations. It feeds on snakes, but may occasionally eat monitor lizards (*Varanus*). Female king cobras construct a nest with a special egg chamber containing up to 40 eggs, and guard the clutch. Even though these snakes have a fearsome reputation, it is unlikely that they ever attack unless provoked. They have been known to enter buildings at forest field stations, causing considerable excitement.

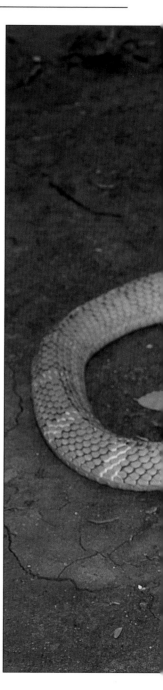

Indraneil Das

Ophiophagus hannah. Close-up of head.

200

Ophiophagus hannah.

Stephen Von Peltz

R.B. Stuebing

Ophiophagus hannah. Juvenile.

Laticaudinae

Laticauda colubrina
Yellow-Lipped Sea Krait

The type locality for this species has been lost, but it is widely distributed in South-east Asia and extends south and eastwards to New Caledonia and the Solomon Islands. In Borneo, it is common on small coastal outcrops or islands. *Lati* = broad, *cauda* = tail; *colubrina* is from *coluber* = snake-like.

Sea kraits are conspicuously sexually dimorphic, so that males are small, rarely much over one metre in length, while females are heavier bodied and up to two metres in total length. The total is about 12–14% of total length in males, less than 12% for females. The pupil is round. There are three prefrontal scales and two internasals. There are 21–25 rows of smooth scales. Ventrals are broad, as in land snakes, and number from 225–243; subcaudals 38–47 (males), 30–35 (females); the anal divided; upper labials 7–8. The top of the head is black, while the top of the snout is bright yellow in juveniles and dirty white to light grey in older adults. The body is completely encircled by black bands which are equal in width along and around the body. The upper lip is whitish or yellow, and the chin and throat are creamy white, bordered in black along the edges of the lower jaw. The upper portion of the body is grey, while the belly is white. The tip of the tail is black in females and whitish in males.

Sea kraits are amphibious, and live in aggregations on small rocky, waterless islands or outcrops all along the coasts of Borneo. They come ashore to seek out thermally favorable microhabitats of about 30–31°C. in order to rest, shed skin, digest their food and mate. They feed in coral reefs on moray (and some Conger) eels. Females lay 7–13 eggs apparently in

R.B. Stuebing

Laticauda colubrina.

grottoes or caves (the eggs have not been found in Borneo). Juveniles can be seen at all times of the year.

Although possessing a venom whose toxicity is similar to that of the cobra, the sea krait is one of the most inoffensive snakes in Borneo, and on land shows no aggressive behaviour. There are no records of a human bite by this species. Nevertheless, it should be treated with respect and not disturbed, since a bite is potentially fatal.

Laticauda laticaudata is a similar species, but in Borneo has so far been recorded only from the Si Amil Islands off the eastern coast of Sabah. It differs in having fewer mid-body scale rows (17), a dark lip and an elongated yellow patch on the jaw extending backwards to the first yellow band on the neck.

Hydrophiinae

The Hydrophiinae includes all the fully aquatic sea snakes of 11 genera known so far from Borneo. Apart from the oar-shaped tail, they are variable in form and habit. Some of them are of relatively small size, with tiny heads (*Microcephalophis gracilis*, *Hydrophis caerulescens*), and others grow quite large (*Leioselasma cyanocincta*, *L. spiralis*). The width of ventral scales is much reduced, and mostly less than twice that of the body scales, or even indistinguishable from the latter. A crease or fold down the middle of the belly is an adaptation allowing hydrophiines to vertically compress the body for swimming. The skin is often loose, with large interspaces that can augment absorption of oxygen from the water. There is, in addition, a saccular lung extension which can reach even into the tail. The upper body scales are either keeled, or have a central bump or tubercle. In some such as *Lapemis curtus*, the ventral scales bear thorny projections. Sea snake diets also vary considerably, as some are specialists (*Aipysurus eydouxii*, most *Hydrophis*) while others such as *Lapemis curtus* feed on many different fish species. Hydrophiine venom is one of the most powerful animal toxins known, though most hydrophiines will not bite without provocation. Provocation can include stepping on them, trying to fend them off vigourously or (for scientists) leaving the snakes in the sun to overheat. Overheated sea snakes are extremely dangerous and they are driven into a frenzy by temperatures above 33°C, which can be rapidly fatal to them.

Aipysurus eydouxii
Beaded Sea Snake

The type specimen is from the Indian Ocean. Though there are several species of this genus in Australian waters, only this one reaches South-east Asia. In Borneo, it has been found in shallow coastal waters in Sabah, and is commonly captured in prawn trawls. *Aipys* from *Aepys,* Greek for high, tall, *urus,* Greek, tail, perhaps referring to the high flattened tail; *eydouxi,* from the name of a French naturalist of the early 19th century. Males and females are similar in size, reaching a maximum total length of slightly less than one metre. The pupil is round. There are 17 rows of smooth scales. Ventrals are broad, as in land snakes, and in Borneo number from 141–149; subcaudals 27–30; anal divided; upper labials 6. The head is dark brown, and the body is of almost the same diameter throughout its length. The body pattern is series of yellowish or cream coloured bands of dark-edged scales that sometimes give a beaded appearance. This is one of the most attractively patterned sea snakes in South-east Asia. This highly specialised snake spends most of its time in shallow waters not far from shore, where it apparently eats only fish eggs.

H. Voris

Aipysurus eydouxii.

205

The fangs are tiny, and there are no records of this species biting humans, but the venom is still dangerous so that this snake should be regarded with great caution.

Enhydrina schistosa
Beaked Sea Snake

The type locality for this species is Tranquebar in India, but it is common in coastal areas throughout South-east Asia. Name derivation — *Enhydris* (in Greek) = water snake; *ina* = a diminutive or small; *schistos* = split or divided, perhaps referring to the cleft in the front portion of the chin in this species.

Enhydrina schistosa is a medium-sized snake, reaching up to about 1.5 metres in total length. There are 49–60 (males) and 51–66 (females) mid-body rows of keeled scales. Ventrals are distinctly visible, not twice as broad as the dorsal scales. Ventrals 239–322; anal divided; upper labials 7–8. The head is slightly elongated, with a squarish snout. The most distinctive feature of this species is the front of the snout/upper lip, which is sharply pointed and

Indraneil Das

Enhydrina schistosa.

206

extends over the edge of the grooved chin. The top of the head and upper portion of the body of adults are greenish-grey, the body with indistinct dark markings. Juveniles are grey with dark banding. The belly is whitish cream in the front part of the body, becoming greenish yellow towards the tail.

Enhydrina schistosa occurs in shallow coastal waters primarily at or near the mouths of muddy rivers or estuaries. It eats a variety of fishes, but mostly marine or estuarine catfish.

The Beaked Sea Snake is a dangerous species, with potent venom and a reputation in Peninsular Malaysia for biting fishermen. Because of its preference for muddy bottoms, it is sometimes trod upon in shallow tidal flats by people who wade barefoot while netting prawns.

Hydrophis brookii
Brooke's Sea Snake

The type specimen is from the coast of Sarawak, and so far all records are from that area of Borneo. The species is named after the English adventurer and Rajah of Sarawak, Sir James Brooke. It has also been found off the coasts of southern Thailand, Peninsular Malaysia, and northern Java.

Hydrophis brookii is a medium-sized sea snake, reaching a maximum length of just over one metre. The head and neck are one-half to one-third the width of the rear half of the body. There are 37–45 scale rows around the body, each scale with a low central keel or tubercle. The ventrals are distinguishable, but less than twice the width of the adjacent rows. Ventrals 328–414; anal divided; upper labials 6, with the third and fourth touching the eye. The top of the head is dark grey with a yellowish band crossing the top of the snout in front of the eyes and curving back along the sides of the head. There is sometimes a short yellow band between the eyes and another towards the rear of the head. The body is grey above and yellowish below, with 60 to 80 dark bands encircling the body. Near the front of the body the bands are uniform in width from the back to the belly, but near the rear of the body they may taper towards the belly. The tail is also banded, with a black tip.

Hydrophis brookii is an uncommon snake in Bornean waters, so that little is known of the habitats or communities in which it lives, though it apparently feeds on eels. It is certainly dangerous and should be treated with the utmost caution.

Hydrophis caerulescens
Blue-Grey Sea Snake

The type locality for this species is the Indian Ocean. It is widely distributed and common in South-east Asia, and in Bornean waters. *Hydro* = Greek *hydor,* water, Greek, *ophis* = snake; *caeruleus* = Latin, sky blue, — *escens* = Latin, becoming.

This sea snake is a small species, reaching 70–80 cm in total length. There are 38–54 rows of strongly keeled scales. Ventrals are about twice the size of the dorsal scales, and can be easily distinguished throughout the length of the body. Ventrals 253–334 ; anal divided; upper labials 7–8. The head and neck are much smaller in diameter compared to the size of the rear half of the body. The top of the head is dark, almost black, and the upper body bluish-grey, generally whitish or slightly yellowish-white below with broad dark bands which encircle the body, tapering slightly towards the belly. The chin is also dark brown, while the sides of the body and belly are yellowish white at mid-body and greyish white towards the tail. The tip of the tail is black.

Hydrophis caerulescens has been caught in small numbers in prawn trawls in shallow coastal waters off northern and western Borneo, but in larger quantities in Marudu Bay (which may indicate a preference for sheltered areas away from the open sea). It apparently feeds mostly on gobies which it seeks out in their burrows in muddy tidal areas. Little else is known of its habits.

This sea snake possesses a dangerous venom. Although the species is not aggressive and has quite a small mouth and tiny fangs, it still can deliver a serious, even fatal bite.

Hydrophis fasciatus
Blunt-Banded Sea Snake

The type locality for this species is the East Indies, and it is widely distributed in South-east Asia. *Fascia(tus)* = Latin, banded.

Hydrophis fasciatus is a small species, reaching slightly more than one metre in total length. There are 47–58 rows of scales with a small tubercle or short keel. Ventrals are slightly less than twice as wide as the dorsal scales, and can be easily distinguished throughout the length of the body. Ventrals 414–514 ; anal divided; upper labials 6–7 (rarely, 5). The head and neck are much smaller in diameter compared to the size of the rear half of the body. The head and neck are dark olive, almost black with a row of pale spots, sometimes elongated to form bars. The upper body is grey with broad dark bands which encircle the body, but the dark colour is abruptly truncated or blunted and much paler on the sides and belly. The chin is dark, while the sides of the body and belly are yellowish white at mid-body and greyish white towards the tail. The tip of the tail is black.

Hydrophis fasciatus has been caught in prawn trawls in coastal waters off Borneo. It apparently feeds on gobies in muddy tidal areas. Little is known of its habits.

This sea snake, like all the others, possesses a highly toxic venom. Although its mouth and fangs are small, the species can deliver a potentially fatal bite.

H. Voris

Hydrophis fasciatus.

Hydrophis klossi
Greater Dusky Sea Snake

The type locality for this species is Kuala Selangor in the Malay Peninsula but it is widely distributed in South-east Asia, though known from only one locality in northern Borneo. The species is named after C.B. Kloss, who made important contributions to Malaysian herpetology in the early part of the 20th century.

Hydrophis klossi is a medium-sized species, reaching about 1.3 metres in total length. There are 31–39 rows of mid-body scales which are smooth or weakly keeled. Ventrals are distinct, and slightly less than twice as wide as the dorsal scales. Ventrals 360–413; anal divided; upper labials 5 (rarely, 6). The head and neck are about one-third the diameter of the rear half of the body. The top of the head is dark olive or brown, with a row of elongated whitish spots. The upper body is grey with broad dark bands which encircle the body, taper only slightly on the sides, retain their dark colour ventrally

Hydrophis klossi.

H. Voris

and are wider than the light-coloured spaces between them. The chin and forepart of the underbody are also dark, while the sides and belly are yellowish-white at mid-body and greyish white towards the tail. The tip of the tail is black.

Hydrophis klossi is relatively rare in Borneo. Little is known of its habits. Although little is known of its behavior and temperament, it should still be regarded as dangerous.

Similar species include *Hydrophis caerulescens* and *H. fasciatus*, both of which have smaller heads in proportion to their bodies (less than one-fourth the diameter of the thickest part of the body), while *H. klossi* has a distinctly larger head

Hydrophis melanosoma
Lesser Dusky Sea Snake

The type locality is unknown for this species. It is widely distributed in South-east Asia, but known from only Brunei Bay in Borneo. *Melanos* = black, *soma* = body.

Hydrophis melanosoma is a medium to large-sized species, reaching about 1.5 metres in total length. There are 37–41 rows of mid-body scales which are keeled in males. Ventrals are slightly less than twice as broad as the body scales. Ventrals 266–368; anal divided; upper labials 6–7 . The head and neck are about one-third the diameter of the rear half of the body. The top of the head is black, sometimes with a light, horseshoe-shaped mark running across the snout and behind the eyes. The black bands completely encircle the body, and are about twice as wide as the spaces between them. On the upper surface, the colour of the interspaces is grey, becoming whitish or yellowish on the belly. The tip of the tail is black.

This species is relatively rare in Borneo, and little is known of its habits. Like most sea snakes, *H. melanosoma* possesses a powerful venom, and should be regarded as dangerous. Similar species include *Hydrophis caerulescens* and *H. fasciatus*, both of which have smaller heads in proportion to their bodies (less than one-fourth the diameter of the thickest part of the body). *Hydrophis klossi* is similar, but is heavier bodied, its black bands are almost of equal width to the interspaces along the sides of the snake and the forepart of the body of *H. klossi* has whitish elongated spots, while *H. melanosoma* is completely banded behind the head.

Hydrophis melanosoma.

Hydrophis ornatus
Ornate Sea Snake

The type specimen of the Ornate Sea Snake is from the Indian Ocean. It is an uncommon species of South-east Asian waters, including coastal Borneo. *Ornatus* = to adorn.

Hydrophis ornatus is a medium-sized sea snake, reaching a maximum length of about one metre. The head and neck are about half the diameter of the widest portion of the body. There 33–55 rows of scales, with the females usually having more rows than the males. The dorsal scales have short keels. The ventrals, about twice the width of the adjacent scales, are distinct the length of the body. Ventrals 209–312, the females with more than the males;

anal divided; upper labials 7 or 8, the third and fourth touching the eye. The head is dark grey to black, lighter on the sides. The body is greyish with many broad, dark bands separated by narrow light interspaces. The bands do not encircle the body. Below the head and body are yellowish white. The end of the tail is black.

This is a rare snake in Bornean waters; its distribution and habits remain largely unknown. It is certainly venomous and dangerous to humans.

Hydrophis ornatus.

H. Voris

Hydrophis torquatus
Garland Sea Snake

The type specimen is from Penang, in Peninsular Malaysia. There is a single record of this species from "Borneo", but since its main distribution lies along the Straits of Malacca and in the Gulf of Thailand, it is possible that the Borneo specimen is either a vagrant or an error. The species name is from the Latin *torques*, a twisted neck chain.

Hydrophis torquatus.

Kerilia jerdoni
Saddle-Backed Sea Snake

The type locality for this species is Madras, India. It is widely distributed in Southeast Asia. The origin of the name is unclear, though the genus may be of Indian derivation. The species was named after a 19th Century field biologist.

Kerilia jerdoni is a medium-sized species, with adults slightly over a metre in total length. There are 21 (sometimes 19) rows of smooth or strongly keeled scales. Ventrals are approximately the same width as the body scales. Ventrals 212–253 ; anal divided; upper labials 6. The snout is sharply tapered, and the head about one-third the diameter of the rear half of the body. The top of the head is dark grey, and there is a black band across the nape. The upper surface of the body is greyish onto the sides, while the belly is whitish or yellowish-white. The chin is dusky. Black bands encircle the body, broad over the midline and tapering rapidly on the belly, giving a saddle-like appearance. On the sides the bands are only about one-third the

214

width of the light interspaces. The tail is black, though many scales have light centres.

Kerilia jerdoni has been caught in small numbers in prawn trawls from shallow coastal waters in northern Borneo. Little is known of its habits. This sea snake, like the other members of its family, should be regarded as dangerous.

Lapemis curtus
Short Sea Snake

The type locality for *Lapemis hardwickii* is listed as East Indies. The latter species is now regarded as a form of *Lapemis curtus*, which has a far broader distribution, from South-east Asia to the Persian Gulf. The species is quite common in the coastal waters of Borneo. The origin of the word *Lapemis* is uncertain though it may be an intentional anagram of *Pelamis* (?); *curtus* = Latin, short. Adults of the Short Sea Snake are about 80–90 cm in total length. There are 25–37 (males), 33–41 (females) rows of hexagonally

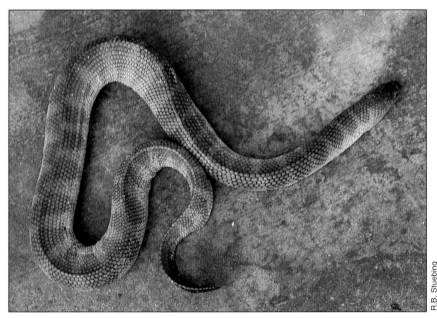

Lapemis curtus.

215

shaped or squarish scales, the lower most rows with a short keel or tubercle, which can form a thorn-like spine in males. Ventrals are not wider than body scales, and irregular. Ventrals 114–186 (males), 141–230 (females); the anal is divided; upper labials 7–8. The head is short and broad, and the body is deeper than wide. The top of the head is brown, with some whitish or yellowish areas in juveniles. The lower lip and sometimes the chin are dusky or brownish. There are bands the entire length of the body, with their broadest parts at the midline, tapering on the sides. The belly is unmarked whitish, or yellowish. The tip of the tail is brown and unmarked, except for irregular light speckling.

Lapemis curtus has been caught in large numbers in prawn trawls at the estuaries of major rivers in Borneo, where it feeds on a wide variety of small fish, and has been known even to take squid. Little is known of its habits apart from its apparent preference for muddy bottoms at the mouths of rivers.

The Short Sea Snake possesses a venom whose toxicity is several times that of a cobra. Although this species is not particularly aggressive, when disturbed or overheated it has been observed to go into a biting frenzy. It should be treated with the utmost caution, and never handled.

Leioselasma cyanocincta
Dusky-Chinned Giant Sea Snake

The type locality for this species is Bangale (Bengal, now Bangladesh), and it is common, though never particularly abundant, in South-east Asia. It shows a similar pattern around Borneo, where it is common in coastal waters. *Leio* = Greek, smooth, *selasma* = Greek, shining; *Cyanos* = dark blue, *cinctus* = belted or girdled.

This sea snake and the related *L. spiralis*, are the longest of the South-east Asian species with adults reaching nearly three metres in total length. There are 37–47 rows of partially or weakly keeled, bluntly pointed scales. Ventrals are approximately twice as wide as the body scales, and regular in shape. Ventrals 292–389; anal divided; upper labials 7–8. The head and neck are slender compared to the rear half of the body. The top of the head is yellowish-green, and the sides yellowish-white. The chin is whitish with dusky or light brownish mottling. Bands encircle the body, black and broadest at the midline, usually tapering and becoming paler on the sides. There may be a black ventral stripe. Occasional specimens have broadening

216

of the bands ventrally on the sides of the body. The belly is mostly whitish, or yellowish, in between the indistinct ventral portions of the bands. The tip of the tail is dark brown.

Leioselasma cyanocincta has been caught in small numbers in prawn trawls in shallow coastal waters in north-western Borneo. The species apparently feeds on eels of the genus *Muraenesox*. Little is known of its habits although it may forage mainly in open water away from river mouths. Although not aggressive, this snake should not be handled as it is dangerously venomous.

Leioselasma spiralis
Blotch-Backed Giant Sea Snake

The type locality for this species is the Indian Ocean. It is uncommon in the coastal waters off Borneo and relatively rare in collections. *Spiralis* = from Latin *spira*, coiled, twisted. *Leioselasma spiralis* grow very large, with adults reaching approximately two metres in total length. There are 33–38 rows of smooth or weakly keeled scales. Ventrals are approximately twice as wide as the body scales, and regular in shape. Ventrals 295–362; anal divided; upper labials 6–8. The head and neck are slender in comparison to

H. Voris

Leioselasma spiralis.

217

the rear half of the body. The top of the head and body are yellowish to yellowish-green, and the sides yellowish-white. The chin is whitish with dusky or light brownish mottling. Narrow bands encircle the body, black and broadest at the midline, sometimes with black dorsal spots between the bands, which usually taper and become much paler towards the belly; there may be a black ventral stripe in young specimens. The belly is mostly whitish, or yellowish, in between the indistinct ventral portions of the bands. The tip of the tail is dark brown.

Leioselasma spiralis has so far not been caught in prawn trawls from shallow coastal waters off Borneo. It has one of the most potent venoms of the group, and though not considered aggressive, is dangerous nonetheless.

Microcephalophis gracilis
Narrow-Headed Sea Snake

The type locality is unknown for this species, and the locality given is simply, "Borneo". The most recent records are from the west coast of Sabah. *Micro* = Latin, tiny, *cephalos* = Greek, head, *ophis* = Greek, snake; *gracilis* = Latin, slender.

This snake reaches about one metre in total length, and is characterised by an extremely small head and slender neck, less than one-quarter the

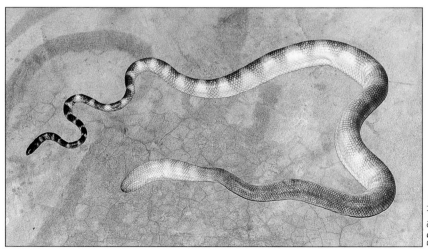

R.B. Stuebing

Microcephalophis gracilis.

218

Microcephalophis gracilis. Close-up of head.

thickness of the rear half of the body. There are 29–37 rows of keeled scales around the thickest part of the body. Ventrals = 212–360, upper labials = 6. The head is black, and the neck marked with dark or black bands with narrow light grey interspaces. The broad black crossbands are indistinct in older specimens , and are tapered and incomplete around the whitish belly. The tail is dark-grey to black.

This species resembles *Hydrophis caerulescens* in both shape and colour, but can be distinguished by its lower number of upper labial scales (6 vs. 7–8 in *H. caerulescens*).

Pelamis platurus
Yellow-Bellied Sea Snake

The type locality is unknown for this widespread pelagic species, which occurs from the South China Sea to the Coasts of Central America. Most records for Borneo are rather old, perhaps because *P. platurus* is mostly found well offshore. (There is a recent record from the beach at Panaga, near Seria in Brunei). "*Pelamis*" is from *pelamys* = Greek, a young tunny. *platys* = Greek, flat; *ouros* = Greek, tail.

Pelamis platyurus reaches about one metre in total length. There are 49–67 mid-body scale rows. Ventrals are irregular in shape and beyond the forepart of the body, not clearly differentiated from the dorsal scales. Ventrals 264–406, divided by a groove ; anal divided; upper labials 7–8. The head

219

shape differs from that of other sea snakes in South-east Asia as it is elongated, and slightly flattened, and almost python-like if viewed from above, while the body is compressed vertically. The neck and body are slender, about one-third to one-half the diameter of the thickest part of the body. The top of the head is dark brown to black above, and yellow below. Tweedie reports the body pattern to be variable, mainly in the width of the black and degree of spotting but the most common one is black above and bright yellow to orange below. The belly is sometimes darker, or can have a row of black spots. The tail is bright yellow, spotted with black.

The Yellow-Bellied Sea Snake is rare in the inshore or coastal areas of Borneo, and so far has not been collected in trawl samples. It may possibly be more common further offshore, well away from the river mouths and reefs that are the habitat of the majority of the Bornean sea snakes. So far, there are few specimens in local collections.

Pelamis platurus is a dangerous snake that should be avoided and not disturbed. Unlike many of the inshore species, it will bite if handled, and the bite can be fatal.

Praescutata viperina [20]
Grey Sea Snake

The type locality is Java, and the species is quite widely distributed, but in South-East Asia known mostly from the Straits of Malacca and the Gulf of Thailand. The only record from Borneo is from western Sarawak. *Prae* = Latin, before, *scutum*, Latin, shield (referring to the head shields); *viperina* = Latin, a small viper or venomous snake.

The total length of this species is about one metre, with males slightly larger than females. There are hexagonal, keeled scales in 37–40 (some up to 50) mid-body rows. Ventrals are unusual, as they are as broad as the dorsal scales in the forepart of the body, and become progressively narrower beyond the midpoint until they are less than half the width of the dorsal scales. Ventrals 226–274 for Peninsular Malaysian specimens; anal divided; upper labials 7–9. The upper labials are separated from the eye by a row of subocular scales. The top of the head is grey to dark grey sometimes with light mottling, and the sides, lips and chin white. Tweedie reports the body

---

[20] *Thalassophina viperina,* according to some references.

pattern to be grey above and whitish below. There may be large, dark vertebral spots in young specimens. The tail is mostly black.

Only one specimen has been recorded from Borneo, from the mouth of the Oya River in western Sarawak more than 80 years ago. There are no recent records, so this species is apparently rather uncommon. Little is known of its ecology in Borneo, but in Thailand, it has been reported to feed mainly on marine invertebrates.

Kolpophis annandalei
Annandale's Sea Snake

The type locality of this species is Pattani Bay, southern Thailand. It has been found in other areas of the Gulf of Thailand. The only Bornean record is of a single specimen collected from Brunei in 1993. *Kolpo* = folded or divided, *ophis* = snake. The species was named after Nelson Annandale who contributed greatly to knowledge of amphibians and reptiles of southern Asia.

Indraneil Das

Kolpophis annandalei.

221

Kolpophis annandalei is a medium-sized sea snake reaching a length of just under one metre. Its upper head shields tend to be fragmented. There is usually an extra pair of shields between the internasals and prefrontals and the rear of the frontal shield is broken into small scales. The head is only slightly narrower than the maximum width of the body. The ventrals, about twice the width of the adjacent scales, are distinct the length of the body. There are 74–93 rows of smooth or weakly keeled scales around the body. Ventrals 320–360; upper labials 9–11, some of the labials fragmented. This species is grey above and yellowish below. The head is dark grey with indistinct lighter mottling. The body has many dark bands that often run together on the back and taper low on the sides.

Very little is known of the biology of this species.

Thalassophis anomalous
Anomalus Sea Snake

This species, originally described from Java, is distributed along the southern coasts of Thailand and Indo-China, the coasts of Java, and the Indonesian archipelago. It has been recorded only twice in Borneo (Sabah and Sarawak), but the records are quite old. *Thalassa* = Greek, the sea ; *ophis* = snake; *anomalus* = deviation, irregular. We have not seen this snake in Borneo, and so the description is based on details given elsewhere.[21]

This is a short, heavy-bodied snake with a short blunt head, attaining a maximum length of about 80 cm. The tail is strongly compressed. The conspicuously keeled scales are in 31–35 rows around the mid-portion of the body. Ventral scales (210–256) are about the same width as those of the body. The shields on the snout and front of the head are irregular and often variably divided into four to five separate scales. The frontal is small and sometimes divided as well. There are 7–8 upper labials, the 3rd to the 5th touching the eye.

The colouration is light grey above, and whitish below, with broad dark bars on the back, which narrow along the sides but often are connected along the centre of the back, and sometimes also encircle the body.

Tweedie reports that this species feeds mainly on eels. Little else is known of its habits, except that it is venomous and potentially dangerous.

---

[21] Cox, M.J. 1991. *The Snakes of Thailand and their Husbandry.*
Tweedie, M.W.F. 1983. *Snakes of Malaya* (3rd ed.).

222

Crotalidae
Pit-viperes

Trimeresurus, *Tropidolaemus*, and *Ovophis* are Asian pit-vipers of the family Crotalidae to which the rattlesnakes belong. Five of the six Bornean species are rather stout-bodied and all possess a wide, triangular head. There is a prominent heat-sensitive pit between the eye and the nostril, which is used both in seeking prey and in defensive behavior. All species are venomous, but some are more dangerous than others. Venom components can vary geographically as well, so that all pit-vipers should be treated with respect, and not disturbed. Their lazy demeanor by day contrasts substantially to their quick aggressiveness at night.

Ovophis chaseni
Kinabalu Brown Pit-viper

The type locality is the village of Kiau, Mount Kinabalu, Sabah. So far as we know, this species has been seen only five times, four on Mount Kinabalu between 915 and 1430 metres above sea level, and once in the Kampong Tagadon area, near the Sunsuron Pass (Crocker Range) at about 1200 metres. The name *Ovophis* may be from *ovum* = egg, and *ophis* = snake; *chaseni* refers to a field biologist and collector (F.N. Chasen) from the early part of this century. This species is an egg layer, unlike the some other pit-vipers in Borneo.

A medium-sized, heavy-bodied pit-viper, with a triangular head typical of the group. Maximum known length is 65 cm. The tail is not prehensile and comprises less than one-seventh of the total length. The head is flat and the snout blunt. Above the eye is a wide supraocular scale separated from its opposite number by three to five scales. There are two or three large scales separating the supraocular scale from the tip of the snout. The second upper

Indraneil Das

Ovophis chaseni. Paratype specimen preserved in Singapore.

labial scale does not border the pit, and the eye is separated from the labial scales by two rows of small scales. The upper head scales are weakly keeled. The upper body scales are strongly keeled in the front part of the body and weakly keeled in the rear half. There are 19 scales rows on the neck, 17 or 19 at mid-body, and 15 near the tail. Ventral scales 131–143 (males), 140 (one female); subcaudals 20–30 (males), 22 (female); upper labials 6. Generally brown, with irregular dark blotches in paired rows down the centre of the back. These gradually change into dark crossbands towards the rear. There is also a row of dark blotches low on the side. The rear of the head has a dark band split by a yellow stripe running from the eye to the neck. The underside is yellowish heavily dusted with grey.

This species has been collected only infrequently, and unfortunately, by persons who did not record any habitat information. Like many montane species, its present restricted distribution is likely an accident of poor sampling. It probably will be found at Mount Mulu, where many Kinabalu montane "endemics" have been found in recent years.

(Opposite). *Trimeresurus borneensis.*

Trimeresurus borneensis
Bornean Leaf-Nosed Pit-viper

This species was originally described from Sarawak, but is widely distributed in all forested parts of Borneo. It is closely related to *Trimeresurus puniceus*, a species occurring in Java, Sumatra, and the Malay Peninsula. *Tri* = three, *mere* = part, and *surus* from *oura* = tail. This name may be derived from the pattern of colours on the caudal scales of several species, giving the impression of a tail divided lengthwise into three equal parts. *Borneensis* = the place of origin.

This pit-viper is thick-bodied as an adult, but almost slender as a juvenile. It has the triangular head typical of pit-vipers. The head has four to six slightly enlarged scales that project, leaf-like over the snout and nostril. Maximum known length is under one metre with a short tail (13–17%); the largest specimen we have seen measured 83 cm. The tail is prehensile. Scales on top of the head are small and smooth; those on the side of the head behind

R.B. Stuebing

Bjorn Lardner

Trimeresurus borneensis. Close-up of head.

the eye are keeled. The supraocular scale above the eye may be divided into two or three scales. The eye, which has a vertical pupil, is separated from the upper labials by several rows of small scales. The body scales are smooth or faintly keeled. At mid-body, there are 21 rows of scales, reducing to 15 rows near the tail. Ventral scales 163–170 (males), 155–163 (females); subcaudals 53–58 (males), 46–51 (females); upper labial scales usually 10 or 11. This pit-viper is brown with black-edged saddles across the back, and a row of light spots low on the sides. The markings become more intense in the rear portion of the body. The only pattern on the head is an oblique yellowish stripe from the eye to the neck. This species is very well-camouflaged, especially when the snake is on the leaf litter of the forest floor. The underside is greyish brown to brown, becoming darker towards the rear. In young snakes the tail is yellow, contrasting sharply with the body colour.

Trimeresurus borneensis is a relatively abundant species of lowland forests up to about 750 m above sea level. We have found juveniles on the forest floor, where they blend well with the leaf litter, even with their bright-coloured tail. Adults are arboreal; we have seen them on prop roots and in holes of tree trunks two to three metres above ground. Juveniles also climb into low vegetation gripping twigs with their prehensile tails. In this position, juveniles often pull their body into a flat coil. They do not hesitate to strike if threatened or disturbed. Two members of our work group have been bitten

226

by young snakes when we unknowingly passed too close during the night. In both cases there were no signs of envenomation. Still, this species must be treated as dangerous. Little is known of the diet. One adult contained mammal hair. We suspect that juveniles feed on small lizards, though that needs confirmation.

Trimeresurus borneensis is generally similar in coloration to the poorly known montane pit-viper, *Ovophis chaseni*, which is also brown. The latter species has larger head scales; there are four or five across the top of the head between the supraocular scales, which are quite large. In *Trimeresurus borneensis* there are 10–12 scales between the supraoculars, which are narrow and rather small.

Trimeresurus malcolmi
Kinabalu Pit-viper

The type locality for this species is Sabah, and specimens are known only from this limited area adjacent to Mount Kinabalu. It occurs at elevations above 1000 metres. The species is named after the famous documenter of South-east Asian herpetofauna, Dr Malcolm Smith.

Stephen Von Peltz

Trimeresurus malcolmi. Close-up of head.

This species is relatively short, the largest specimen attaining a total length of just over one metre with the tail 16–18% of total length. It is a stout-bodied pit-viper with a relatively narrow head. The eye is small, and the pupil is vertical. There are 19 rows of keeled scales at mid-body. Ventrals are 169–173 (males) and 168–174 (females); paired subcaudals 73–81 (males) and 61–64 (females). This species is similar in appearance to the Sumatran Pit-Viper (*Trimeresurus sumatranus*), but differs in possessing a striking pattern of bright green dots on a black background. The upper surfaces of the body are black, tending to form indistinct transverse bands, each scale on the head and back with green triangle occupying the posterior portion of each dorsal scale. The ventrals have a light green leading edge, and a dark posterior border. The tail pattern consists of rows of uniform, parallel black scales, each with a red spot. The subcaudals are light green, edged with black.

Little is known of the habits of *T. malcolmi* since only a few specimens have been collected. The areas where the snakes were found between 1000 and 1600 metres on Kinabalu are covered by oak forests, primary within the

R.B. Stuebing

Trimeresurus malcolmi.

228

park boundaries, but disturbed on the outside. All specimens were found on the forest floor, or on roads adjacent to such habitats. The diet is unknown, but a specimen kept alive by Tan Fui Lian and Thomas Yussop in Kinabalu Park for several years fed on small mammals such as rats and ground squirrels.

Trimeresurus popeorum [22]
Pope's Pit-viper

This species was originally described from northeastern India, but has been found in highlands in Thailand, Peninsular Malaysia, Sumatra, and Borneo. It has been recorded from montane areas of Sabah and Sarawak, but

---

[22] Malcolm Smith, the describer of this species, states that the spelling "popeiorum" was a typographical error not present in his original manuscript.

Trimeresurus popeorum.

R.B. Stuebing

R.B. Stuebing

not yet from similar elevations in Kalimantan. The species was named after Clifford H. Pope, an eminent herpetologist specializing in the fauna of eastern Asia.

Trimeresurus popeorum is relatively slender for a pit-viper, but has the typical wide, triangular head of the group. The head is flat and the snout blunt. Maximum length is less than one metre; the largest Bornean specimen we have seen measured 76 cm. The tail, which is prehensile, makes up about one-sixth of the total. Scales on top of the head are smooth, those on the body are smooth or very weakly keeled. The supraocular scale is undivided. Two scales lie between the eye and the nasal scale. The eye is separated from the upper labials by a row of small scales and a row of large scales. There are 21 rows of scales at mid-body, the number reducing to 15 before the tail. Ventral scales 154–159; subcaudals 63; upper labials 9 or 10. This species is entirely bright green, except for a white line running the length of the body and tail low on the side, on adjacent halves of the first two scale rows. In some individuals there is a row of small white spots down the centre of the back. The belly is a bit lighter than the sides.

All the Bornean records are from lower montane forest, around 1000–1150 m above sea level. However, in Thailand *Trimeresurus popeorum* occurs below 500 m. This snake usually is seen in low vegetation, clinging to small branches or twigs. Juveniles feed on lizards. Although the diet of adults is unknown, probably they feed on small mammals the way other, related species do. As is the case for most pit-vipers, this species tends to be fairly sluggish during the day, but active and much more likely to bite at night. Probably sensing the heat, it will strike at a headlamp beam.

Trimeresurus sumatranus
Sumatran Pit-viper

The type locality is Sumatra, but this species occurs throughout the Sunda Region. It is widely distributed in Borneo at low elevations, and on islands. The specific name is derived from the type locality.

The Sumatran Pit-viper is thick-bodied, and reaches a maximum length of about 1.3 metres, with the prehensile tail about 15% of the total. The head is large and triangular, much broader than the rather slim neck. Scales on top

(Opposite). *Trimeresurus popeorum.*

R.B. Stuebing

Trimeresurus sumatranus. Close-up of head.

of the head are smooth, and the supraocular scales are large and conspicuous. There are 21 rows of scales at mid-body and 17–19 just before the tail. The anal plate is undivided. Ventrals 183–190 (males), 182–191 (females); subcaudals 57–66 (males), 59–64 (females); upper labials 7–10. Adults are various shades of green with dark, indistinct crossbands. The scales of the back are green with with black edges, forming the bands which become more pronounced with age. The underside is light greenish-yellow, and the tail is reddish brown. Juveniles are entirely green with a red tail.

This species is common in lowland forest, and often found sleeping up to half a metre off the ground in small rattans or other shrubs. It is abundant on some of the small islands off Sabah's west coast. Sumatran Pit-vipers are extremely sluggish, and appear to be asleep most of the day. At night, however they can be extremely energetic and thus more dangerous, since they do have the ability to inject a rather large quantity of venom. The diet is mainly small birds and mammals.

Tropidolaemus wagleri
Wagler's Pit-viper

The type locality is Sumatra, but this species occurs from southern Thailand to Sumatra, Borneo, Sulawesi, and the Philippine Islands. It is widely distributed in Borneo at low elevations. *Tropidos* = ridge or keel, *laemus* = throat, referring to the strongly keeled scales of the throat; *Wagler* = an early collector in the East Indies.

Indraneil Das

Tropidolaemus wagleri. Close-up of head. Subadult.

R.B. Stuebing

Like many of the pit-vipers, this species is thick-bodied as an adult but rather slender as a juvenile. Maximum length is just under one metre, with the tail accounting for about one-seventh of the total. The tail is prehensile. The head is large, triangular, and steep-sided, much wider than the fore part of the body. Scales on top of the head are small and strongly keeled. The supraocular scales are scarcely larger than adjoining scales. Scales on the throat and side of the head are larger and strongly keeled. One to three rows of scales separate the eye from the upper labial scales. The body scales are weakly keeled. There are 21–23 rows of scales at mid-body and 17–19 just before the tail. The anal plate is undivided. Ventrals 142–150 (males), 139–148 (females); subcaudals 50–54 (males), 46–54 (females); upper labials 7–9. Adults are black above grading into green below. The scales of the back are black with scattered small green spots; the green becomes more extensive and scales at mid-side are green with black edges. Superimposed on that pattern are vertical green bars. The underside is lighter green. Juveniles are entirely green with a red-edged white line from the snout through the eye to the rear of the head. The side of the body has red-edged white vertical bars.

This is one of the commonest pit-vipers in Borneo. It is abundant in lowland forests and secondary growth. It has a reputation for being rather docile, but can still inflict a painful, if not fatal bite.

(Opposite). *Tropidolaemus wagleri.* juvenile.

APPENDIX I. Local names for Bornean snakes

SPECIES	ENGLISH NAME	MALAY
Acrochordus javanicus	Common file snake	pelaik
Ahaetulla prasina	Green vine snake	ular bunga
Amphiesma flavifrons	White-nosed water snake	ular hidung putih
Anomochilus, Cylindrophis	Pipe snake	ulartanah
Boiga dendrophila	Yellow-ringed cat snake	tetak emas,
Boiga cynodon	Dog-toothed cat snake	ular telor
Bungarus fasciatus	Banded krait	katam, buku tebu
Cerberus rynchops	Dog-faced water snake	(birang)
Chrysopelea paradisi	Paradise tree snake	ular petola
Dendrelaphis caudolineatus	Common bronzeback	ular padang
Dendrelaphis pictus	Elegant bronzeback	ular lidi
Elaphe flavolineata	Common racer	ular sawa
Gonyosoma oxycephalum	Grey-tailed racer	ular pucuk
Maticora intestinalis	Coral snake	ular tedung babi and ular tali kasut
Naja sumatrana	Black cobra	ular senduk

SNAKES OF BORNEO - Addenda and corrigenda

New Bornean records: *Oligodon annulifer* has recently been found in Brunei and Kalimantan, *Opisthotropis typica* in Brunei, and *Dendrelaphis striatus* in Kalimantan. A doubtful record exists for Elapoidis fusca from "northern Borneo."

p. 3: *Ophisaurus buettikoferi* (corrected spelling).

p. 28 *Trimeresurus wagleri* = *Tropidolaemus wagleri*

pp. 42-43: Footnotes to the Key:
- Couplet 36b. "Scales keeled". This includes *Stegonotus borneensis* which possesses weak keels at the outer edge of its ventral scales, although its dorsal scales are smooth.
- Couplet 42b. "Head not as above". This couplet should lead to number 44, and not number 47.

pp. 62-63: *Cylindrophis ruffus* is reported to be a specialized predator of snakes.

pp. 80-81. *Xenelaphis hexagonotus* is in the Subfamily Colubrinae, not the Xenodermatinae

pp. 91-92: The type locality for *Cerberus rynchops*: is Ganjam (Orissa State, India)

p. 93: The correct plate for p. 93 is *Enhydris plumbea*, above.

pp. 190-191: " *Bungarus*" is derived from the Telugu "bungarum pambah/pamu" meaning "golden snake". The type locality for *Bungarus fasciatus*, given as "Bengal", is actually "Mansoor Cotta, located near Ganjam in Orissa State, India.

p. 199-200: *Ophiophagus hannah* : Type locality = "Sunderbans" (near Kolkatta, W. Bengal State, India). The word "hannah" is derived from Greek, meaning "forest nymph".

pp. 225-226: Most old records for *Trimeresurus borneensis* actually referred to as *T. puniceus*.

DUSUN	MURUT	IBAN
—	—	paiie
timpakapaka	mongkostabu	bungai
singgumumu	nangahluba	—
lomok	angui-angui	untop
masalong	nauksalong	bangkit
kodou-ulang	tungkis	—
pomolong	—	kengkang tebu
tamburukoi	—	—
sandai	timbulus	—
deriasu	kuririas	—
timpakapaka	mongkostabu	meresian
kodou-ulang	oloi	—
mansak punti	timpahasan	ular mati iko
rusukan	sanawali	—
belinatong	anunumpi	

Oligodon octolineatus	Striped kukri snake	
Ophiophagus hannah	King cobra	ular tedung
Python reticulatus	Reticulate python	ular sawa batik
Python curtus	Short / Blood python	ular sawa darah
Trimeresurus sumatranus *Tropidolaemus wagleri*	Pit-viper	ular kapak
Xenelaphis hexagonotus	Malaysian Brown snake	—
Xenochrophis trianguligera	Orange-necked water snake	ular air
Zaocys fuscus	Giant forest racer?	—

—	—	emparo
tomumuho	mantakah	belalang
lopung	malawor	ular sawa
—	—	rippong
babakusui	timpahasan	ular beliong, engkrudu
—	—	beluai
singgumumu	angngangarui	—
kodou-ulang	oloi	—

Acknowledgements

We are grateful to C.L. Chan, Indraneil Das, Bjorn Lardner, Harold Voris, Stephen Von Peltz, John Murphy, Jimmy Omar, Au Kam Wah, Ralph Cutter, D.R. Karns, A. Lamb, Francis Lim, W.M. Poon, D. Wechsler and Yong Hoi Sen for permission to use their fine photographs.

Our work on the Bornean snakes has received financial support from the Marshall Field III Fund and the Karl P. Schmidt Fund of the Field Museum of Natural History, and the John D. and Catherine T. MacArthur Foundation. Additional support was also provided by International Tropical Timber Organization (ITTO), Universiti Kebangsaan Malaysia Sabah, Sabah Parks, Sabah Museum, Sarawak Museum, Zoological Reference Collection of the National University of Singapore, and Sarawak Forest Department.

We would like to thank Ghazally Ismail, Lamri Ali, Francis Liew, Eric Wong, Patricia Regis, Cheong Ek Choon, James Dawos Mamit, Barney Chan, Paul Chai, Charles Leh, Sapuan Ahmad, Alim Biun, Paul Yambun, Danson Kandaung, Freddie Julus, Frederick Francis, Patrick Francis, Lucy Kimsui, Awang Latiff Mohammed, Lagani Sahid, Dennis Ikon, Khamis Selamat, Taib Jainudin, Shahbudin Hj. Sabky, Abd. Hamid Ahmad, Anna Wong, Albert Lo, Engkamat Lading, Matius Angkangon, David Labang, Gaun Sering, Saifuddin Senawi, Mabong Utau, Patrick David, Peter Ng, Kelvin Lim and George McDuffie. Thanks also to Clara Simpson of Field Museum who assisted in scanning of the figures and Cheng Jen Wai of Natural History Publications (Borneo) for editing the photographs.

Finally, we are grateful to our families for their patience and support in the writing of this book.

Selected References

Cox, M. (1991). *The Snakes of Thailand and Their Husbandry*. Krieger Publishing, Malabar, FL.

Dunson, W.A. (ed.) (1975). *The Biology of Sea Snakes*. Univ. Park Press, Baltimore (MD).

Greene, H.W. (1997). *Snakes: The Evolution of Mystery in Nature*. University of California Press. 351 pp.

Haile, N.S. (1958). The Snakes of Borneo with a key to the species. *Sar. Mus. Journ.* 8: 743–771.

Inger, R.F. and Tan Fui Lian (1996). *The Natural History of Amphibians and Reptiles in Sabah*. Natural History Publications (Borneo), Kota Kinabalu. 101 pp.

Inger, R.F. and H. Marx (1965). The Systematics and Evolution of the Oriental Colubrid Snakes of the genus *Calamaria. Fieldiana: Zoology* 49: 1–304.

Lim, F. and M. Lee (1989). *Fascinating Snakes of Southeast Asia: An Introduction*. Tropical Press Sdn. Bhd., Kuala Lumpur.

Manthey, U. and W. Grossmann (1997). *Amphibien & Reptilien Shdostasiens*. Natur und Tier Verlag, Berlin. 512 pp.

Murphy, J.C., H.K. Voris and D.R. Karns (1994). A Field Guide and Key to the Snakes of the Danum Valley. *Bull. Chicago Herp. Soc.* 29(7): 133–151

Siegel, R.A. and J.T. Collins (eds.) (1993). *Snakes: Ecology and Behavior*. McGraw Hill, Inc., New York. 414 pp.

Siegel, R.A., J.T. Collins and S. Novak (eds.) (1987). *Snakes: Ecology and Evolutionary Biology*. McGraw Hill, Inc., New York. 529 pp.

Stuebing, R.B. (1991). A Checklist of the Snakes of Borneo. *Raffles Bull. Zool.* 39(2): 323–362.

Stuebing, R.B. (1994). A Checklist of the Snakes of Borneo: Addenda and corrigenda. *Raffles Bull. Zool.* 42(4): 931–936.

Tweedie, M.W.F. (1983). *The Snakes of Malaya.* Singapore National Printers, Singapore. 167 pp.

Index

E

F

G

Spotted   104
Striped   106

L

Lanthonotus borneensis   4
Lapemis   8
Lapemis curtus   13, 19, 23, 28, 49, 204, 215
   hardwickii   215, 216
Laticauda colubrina   8, 13, 19, 20, 21, 22, 23, 28, 32, 48, 202, 203
   laticaudata   13, 204
Laticaudinae   7, 13, 21, 202
leather   32
Leioselasma   8,
Leioselasma cyanocincta   13, 19, 49, 204, 216
   spiralis   13, 49, 204, 217, 218
Lepturophis borneensis   10, 43, 96
Liopeltis   20, 154, 196
Liopeltis baliodeirus   12, 47, 154, 155
   longicauda   12, 46, 143, 154, 156, 157
   tricolor   12, 47, 154, 158
Litter Snake, Mocquard's   161
   Ring-Necked   159
   Striped   162
   White-Lipped   163
Lloyd, Peter   34
Lycodon   98
Lycodon albofuscus   10, 98, 120
   aulicus   10, 43, 99, 100
   effraenis   10, 43, 100, 101
   subcinctus   10, 43, 101, 102, 120
Lycodontinae   6, 10, 96

M

Macropisthodon   7
Macropisthodon flaviceps   12, 47, 172–174
   rhodomelas   12, 48, 175, 176
Maticora   7, 17, 105, 133

P

R

S

T

X

Z

Other titles by *Natural History Publications (Borneo)*

For more information, please contact us at

Natural History Publications (Borneo) Sdn. Bhd.
A913, 9th Floor, Wisma Merdeka
P.O. Box 13908, 88846 Kota Kinabalu, Sabah, Malaysia
Tel: 088-233098 Fax: 088-240768 e-mail: chewlun@tm.net.my

Mount Kinabalu: Borneo's Magic Mountain—an introduction to the natural history of one of the world's great natural monuments *by* K.M. Wong & C.L. Chan

Enchanted Gardens of Kinabalu: A Borneo Diary *by* Susan M. Phillipps

A Colour Guide to Kinabalu Park *by* Susan K. Jacobson

Kinabalu: The Haunted Mountain of Borneo *by* C.M. Enriquez (Reprint)

A Walk through the Lowland Rainforest of Sabah *by* Elaine J.F. Campbell

In Brunei Forests: An Introduction to the Plant Life of Brunei Darussalam *by* K.M. Wong (Revised edition)

The Larger Fungi of Borneo *by* David N. Pegler

Pitcher-plants of Borneo *by* Anthea Phillipps & Anthony Lamb

Nepenthes of Borneo *by* Charles Clarke

Nepenthes of Sumatra and Peninsular Malaysia *by* Charles Clarke

The Plants of Mount Kinabalu 3: Gymnosperms and Non-orchid Monocotyledons *by* John H. Beaman & Reed S. Beaman

Dendrochilum of Borneo *by* Jeffrey J. Wood

Slipper Orchids of Borneo *by* Phillip Cribb

The Genus Paphiopedilum (Second edition) *by* Phillip Cribb

Orchids of Sumatra *by* J.B. Comber

Gingers of Peninsular Malaysia and Singapore *by* K. Larsen, H. Ibrahim, S.H. Khaw & L.G. Saw

Aroids of Borneo *by* Alistair Hay & Peter C. Boyce

Mosses and Liverworts of Mount Kinabalu *by* Jan P. Frahm, Wolfgang Frey, Harald Kürschner & Mario Manzel

Birds of Mount Kinabalu, Borneo *by* Geoffrey W.H. Davison

The Birds of Borneo (Fourth edition)
by Bertram E. Smythies (Revised by Geoffrey W.H. Davison)

The Birds of Burma (Fourth edition) *by* Bertram E. Smythies

Proboscis Monkeys of Borneo *by* Elizabeth L. Bennett & Francis Gombek

The Natural History of Orang-utan *by* Elizabeth L. Bennett

The Systematics and Zoogeography of the Amphibia of Borneo
by Robert F. Inger (Reprint)

A Field Guide to the Frogs of Borneo *by* Robert F. Inger & Robert B. Stuebing

The Natural History of Amphibians and Reptiles in Sabah
by Robert F. Inger & Tan Fui Lian

Marine Food Fishes and Fisheries of Sabah *by* Chin Phui Kong

Layang Layang: A Drop in the Ocean
by Nicolas Pilcher, Steve Oakley and Ghazally Ismail

Phasmids of Borneo *by* Philip E. Bragg

The Dragon of Kinabalu and other Borneo Stories *by* Owen Rutter (Reprint)

Land Below the Wind *by* Agnes N. Keith (Reprint)

Three Came Home *by* Agnes N. Keith (Reprint)

Forest Life and Adventures in the Malay Archipelago *by* Eric Mjoberg (Reprint)

A Naturalist in Borneo *by* Robert W.C. Shelford (Reprint)

Twenty Years in Borneo *by* Charles Bruce (Reprint)

With the Wild Men of Borneo *by* Elizabeth Mershon (Reprint)

Kadazan Folklore (*Compiled and edited by* Rita Lasimbang)

An Introduction to the Traditional Costumes of Sabah
(*eds.* Rita Lasimbang & Stella Moo-Tan)

Manual latihan pemuliharaan dan penyelidikan hidupan liar di lapangan
by Alan Rabinowitz (*Translated by* Maryati Mohamed)

Etnobotani *by* Gary J. Martin (*Translated by* Maryati Mohamed)